MERRIAM-WEBSTER'S
TALK LIKE AN EXPERT
DINOSAURS

Ellen-Thérèse Lamm would like to express great appreciation to Dr. David J. Varricchio, John R. "Jack" Horner, Roger Worthen, Larry Hiller, Dorie Green, Rebecca Lamm, and Sharon Budney for their excellent advice. Special thanks also to dinosaur-digging colleagues around the world whose dedication and determination has led to these fascinating investigations and outstanding discoveries.

Merriam-Webster Kids is an imprint of Merriam-Webster Inc., published in collaboration with What on Earth Publishing.

First published in the United States in 2022

Contributors:
Ellen-Thérèse Lamm, Consultant Editor; Stephanie Warren Drimmer, Writer; Daniel Long, Illustrator

Ellen-Thérèse Lamm is a Montana State University (MSU) employee, working for over 30 years as the Museum of the Rockies' Histology Lab Manager in the Paleontology Department. Her role as Consultant Editor of *Merriam-Webster's Talk Like an Expert: Dinosaurs* is separate from her employment, and this publication is not sponsored by or affiliated with MSU.

Staff for this book
Merriam-Webster Inc.: Linda Wood, Senior Editor; Em Vezina, Director of Editorial Operations; Josh Guenter, Pronunciation Editor

Encyclopaedia Britannica: Alison Eldridge, Managing Editor; John P. Rafferty, Editor of Earth and Life Sciences; Michele Rita Metych, Fact Checking Supervisor; Will Gosner, Fact Checker

What on Earth Publishing: Nancy Feresten, Publisher; Natalie Bellos, Editorial Director; Max Bisantz, Executive Editor; Meg Osborne, Editor; Andy Forshaw, Art Director; Andy Mansfield, Art Director and Designer; Daisy Symes, Designer

WonderLab Group, LLC: Kate Hale, Project Manager; Jen Agresta, Glossary Writer; Hillary Leo, Picture Researcher; Lori Merritt, Copy Editor; Susan Hom, Proofreader

Library of Congress Cataloging-in-Publication Data available upon request
First Edition, 2022

ISBN: 9780877791195

Printed and bound in Canada
FC/Altona, Manitoba, Canada/10/2022
10 9 8 7 6 5 4 3 2

MIX
Paper from
responsible sources
FSC® C016245

MERRIAM-WEBSTER'S
TALK LIKE AN EXPERT

DINOSAURS

400 words for budding paleontologists

CONSULTANT EDITOR **Ellen–Thérèse Lamm**
ILLUSTRATOR **Daniel Long**

CONTENTS

TRICERATOPS

DINOSAUR DEFINITIONS

Throughout this book, you'll see hundreds of awesome words to help you understand the language of dinosaurs. Some words are so important to dinosaur science that they're featured in a special box on the page. Other key words are also in **bold**. You can find the official Merriam-Webster definitions of all these words and many more in the Paleontology Dictionary on page 52.

FOREWORD

Millions of years ago, **dinosaurs** lived across our planet. Some dinosaurs were powerful and plated while others were fast and feathered. Some ate plants— and some ate each other! For about 165 million years, dinosaurs were the most successful animals on Earth. But then, about 66 million years ago, nearly all of these fantastic beasts went away forever.

Have you ever wondered how we know about these long-dead creatures? It is because they left behind clues about their lives: **fossils**. Today, experts called **paleontologists** study these remains. They examine all kinds of life forms that emerged long ago, from plants and microbes to beetles and butterflies, from swimming sea creatures to flying reptiles all the way to *Coelophysis* (my favorite dinosaur, which you can meet on page 11).

Some experts study fossilized dinosaur bones. Others study teeth, skin, or even dinosaur poop! Still others, like me, use microscopes to look at the insides of fossils. The evidence all paleontologists gather helps answer questions about the lives of dinosaurs. Find out more about amazing paleontology careers on pages 48–49.

We paleontologists use special words to talk about our work. Using these words allows us to communicate, work together, and even debate about discoveries. These words also help dinosaur fans understand our work so they can learn more about these fascinating animals. This book will introduce you to the language of dinosaur science, so when it is your turn, you can talk like an expert!

Ellen-Thérèse Lamm
Paleohistologist
Museum of the Rockies, Montana State University

DINOSAUR
DYE-noh-sor
(noun) any of a group of mostly land-dwelling reptiles that lived millions of years ago

FOSSIL
FAH-sul
(noun) a trace or print or the remains of a plant or animal of a past age preserved in earth or rock

PALEONTOLOGIST
pay-lee-ahn-TAH-luh-jist
(noun) a person who studies life from the past using fossil remains

MEET THE DINOSAURS
Travel Back in Time

The first dinosaurs appeared on Earth about 240 million
years ago. They were small in size, some no bigger than
housecats. But before long, dinosaurs had taken over
the planet. They walked on every part of Earth's land—
and some even flew in the skies! They dominated life
on Earth for millions of years.

DINOSAURS WERE ALL DIFFERENT

There were hundreds of different **species** of
dinosaurs, each with unique features and
behaviors. Many of these traits were
adaptations that helped dinosaurs
survive and thrive. Some dinosaurs had
sharp eyesight that helped them hunt their
prey. Others grew to enormous sizes, towering
above the rest. There were dinosaurs with
spiked tails, curved claws, and sharp **horns**.
And of course, some had huge mouths
filled with teeth that allowed them to eat
almost anything they could find!

VELOCIRAPTOR

SCALES

FEATHERS

THEY HAD SCALES...AND FEATHERS!

Like their **reptile** relatives, all dinosaurs had **scales**. These small,
hard plates grow out of an animal's skin and provide its body
with protection. But scientists now know that some dinosaurs
had more than scaly skin—many sported feathers, too! The first
feathers probably helped dinosaurs keep warm and attract mates.
Eventually, some dinosaurs used their feathers to take flight.

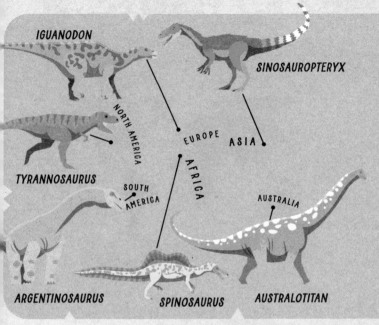

IGUANODON

SINOSAUROPTERYX

NORTH AMERICA

EUROPE

ASIA

TYRANNOSAURUS

SOUTH AMERICA

AFRICA

AUSTRALIA

ARGENTINOSAURUS

SPINOSAURUS

AUSTRALOTITAN

THEY LIVED AROUND THE WORLD

Ancient dinosaur remains have been discovered on all seven major landmasses, or **continents**—even in Antarctica! And a few places on Earth are hotbeds of discovery, where huge numbers of species have been unearthed. *Stegosaurus, Triceratops, Tyrannosaurus,* and more have been discovered in western North America. China is home to many feathered dinosaurs such as *Sinosauropteryx.* And a huge variety of long-necked dinosaurs come from all over South America.

THEY MIGHT HAVE BEEN WARM-BLOODED

Books and movies used to depict dinosaurs a bit like big clumsy lizards. Scientists assumed dinosaurs were **ectotherms** *(EK-tuh-thermz),* or cold-blooded animals. These animals use their environment, such as the heat from the Sun, to warm their bodies. Most modern-day reptiles are cold-blooded. But now, scientists know that many dinosaur species ran fast, swam, and flew. These behaviors are all traits of **endotherms** *(EN-doh-thermz),* or warm-blooded animals—creatures that produce heat within their bodies. Were dinosaurs warm-blooded, cold-blooded, or a mix of both? Scientists are still figuring it out!

FOSSIL

Spinosaurus had a large sail on its back that may have helped it control its body temperature.

FOSSIL EVIDENCE SHOWS HOW THEY LIVED

How do we know so much about dinosaurs? Over the millions of years since dinosaurs lived, some of the bones, teeth, eggs, footprints, and other evidence of their existence slowly turned to stone in a process called **fossilization**. Now, dinosaur experts called paleontologists search for these fossils and study them in laboratories. Fossil evidence allows them to discover not only what some dinosaurs looked like, but what they ate, how they raised their young, and even what they sounded like!

EARTH ON THE MOVE
Dinosaurs in a Changing World

When dinosaurs roamed, Earth looked very different from how it does today. At the beginning of the age of dinosaurs, nearly all of the planet's land was joined together in one giant **supercontinent** called **Pangea** *(pan-JEE-uh)*. By the end of the dinosaurs' reign, that land had separated into smaller landmasses called continents.

A PLANET IN MOTION

How did that happen? The **theory** of **plate tectonics** says that Earth's surface is made up of giant pieces that fit together like a jigsaw puzzle. Heat traveling through the planet's interior causes the plates to move very slowly: sometimes toward each other and sometimes away from each other.

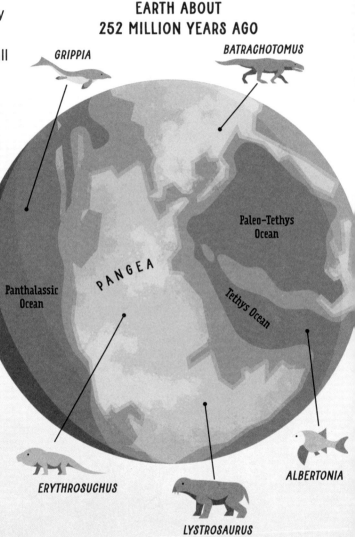

EARTH ABOUT 252 MILLION YEARS AGO

GRIPPIA

BATRACHOTOMUS

Paleo-Tethys Ocean

Panthalassic Ocean

PANGEA

Tethys Ocean

ERYTHROSUCHUS

LYSTROSAURUS

ALBERTONIA

THE EARTH'S TECTONIC PLATES TODAY

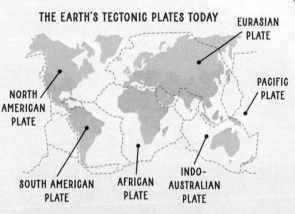

EURASIAN PLATE

PACIFIC PLATE

NORTH AMERICAN PLATE

SOUTH AMERICAN PLATE

AFRICAN PLATE

INDO-AUSTRALIAN PLATE

Over the millions of years that dinosaurs were alive, this motion totally transformed the planet. The plates that formed Pangea moved apart, causing the land to crack and separate. Seawater filled in the gaps, creating new oceans and forming new coastlines. This slowly shifting landscape meant big changes for dinosaurs.

LIFE ON PANGEA

When the earliest dinosaurs appeared, they could make their way to every part of Earth's land. Similar species lived in places from what is now the United States to China to Antarctica. The enormous size of Pangea made it nearly impossible for cool sea breezes and rain to reach the interior, so much of the land was dry and hot. These vast deserts made survival there tough. Therefore, most early dinosaurs lived near the edges of the oceans or other water sources.

PLATE TECTONICS

PLAYT-tek-TAH-niks

(noun) a scientific theory that Earth's surface is made of very large sections that move very slowly

DINOSAUR TIME

The age that saw the rise of the dinosaurs spanned 186 million years. Scientists call this span of time the **Mesozoic Era**, and they divide it into three **periods**. Dinosaurs emerged in the Triassic Period and came to dominate life on Earth during the Jurassic Period. But their rule ended when a space rock the size of a small city slammed into the planet. This triggered an **extinction** event that closed out the Cretaceous Period 66 million years ago (MYA), ending the Mesozoic Era and destroying more than three-quarters of all life on the planet.

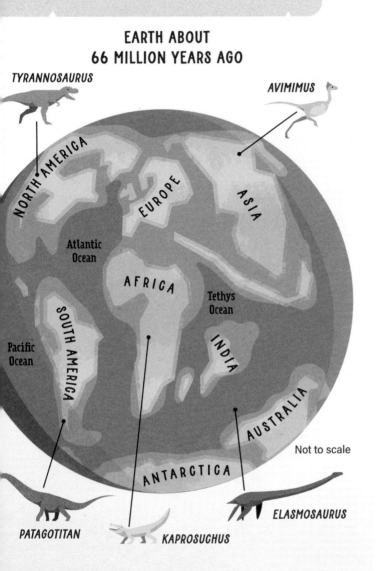

EARTH ABOUT 66 MILLION YEARS AGO

TYRANNOSAURUS

AVIMIMUS

NORTH AMERICA

EUROPE

ASIA

Atlantic Ocean

AFRICA

Tethys Ocean

SOUTH AMERICA

INDIA

Pacific Ocean

AUSTRALIA

ANTARCTICA

Not to scale

ELASMOSAURUS

PATAGOTITAN

KAPROSUCHUS

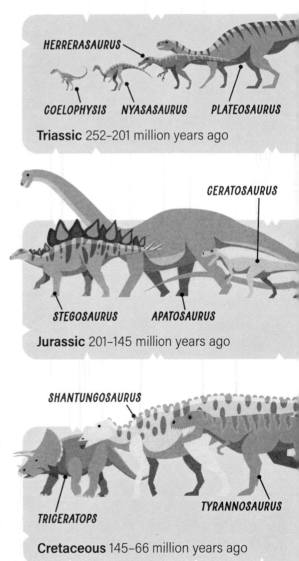

HERRERASAURUS

COELOPHYSIS   NYASASAURUS   PLATEOSAURUS

Triassic 252–201 million years ago

CERATOSAURUS

STEGOSAURUS   APATOSAURUS

Jurassic 201–145 million years ago

SHANTUNGOSAURUS

TRICERATOPS

TYRANNOSAURUS

Cretaceous 145–66 million years ago

THE BREAKUP

As Pangea broke apart, the **climate** became warm and wet. Dinosaurs adapted to their new environments and eventually evolved into many new species fit for living in Earth's new swamps and forests. And because the continents became separated by oceans, different species evolved on different continents. This meant that by the end of the age of dinosaurs, there was an enormous variety of different types, from a speedy *Velociraptor* to a towering *Apatosaurus* to a toothy *Tyrannosaurus rex*.

DAWN OF THE DINOSAURS
Triassic Period

The age of the dinosaurs began in the Triassic. Before dinosaurs appeared, the ground cracked and spewed out lava for hundreds of thousands of years. Nine out of every ten species on the planet went extinct. The mass wipeout created room for the surviving creatures to thrive. Among the survivors were early **archosaurs**, which included the relatives of pterosaurs, crocodiles…and dinosaurs. These animals took over new environments and adapted to new surroundings. Eventually, the very first dinosaurs evolved.

ARCHOSAUR
AHR-kuh-sor
(noun) any of a class of reptiles that includes pterosaurs, crocodiles, and dinosaurs

THEROPOD
THEER-uh-pahd
(noun) any of a group of meat-eating dinosaurs that walked on two legs, had hips positioned like those of lizards, and had hollow long bones and usually small forelimbs

Prehistoric Plants
Pangea's lakes, streams, and coastal areas were moist and filled with plant life. **Gymnosperms** *(JIM-nuh-spermz)*, or non-flowering plants that reproduce with seeds, flourished. Forests were filled with primitive pines, low-lying **ferns**, mosses, and plant species that are still living today, such as *Ginkgo* trees and **Cycads**.

PLATEOSAURUS

CYCAD

PLACERIAS
This creature was a type of **dicynodont** *(dye-SIN-oh-dahnt)*, a group of animals with beaks and tusks. It ate plants and lived near water.

252–201 MYA

TRIASSIC TIMELINE*
Lasting just over 50 million years, the Triassic Period was filled with fantastic firsts:

*All dates are approximate

250 MYA: FIRST MARINE REPTILES EMERGE

246 MYA: FIRST TRUE ARCHOSAURS APPEAR

243 MYA: *NYASASAURUS*, FIRST KNOWN DINOSAUR APPEARS

230 MYA: PANGEA BEGINS TO BREAK APART

250 MYA   240 MYA   230 M

ARAUCARIOXYLON

Trees that resembled modern **conifers**, or pine trees.

MORMOLUCOIDES

An ancient **insect** that resembled a modern-day dragonfly.

Early Dinosaurs

This fast-moving, sharp-toothed dinosaur may have hunted in packs. *Coelophysis* was one of the oldest dinosaurs whose fossils have been found in North America. It was an early **theropod**, a group of dinosaurs that would eventually include *T. rex*.

GINKGO

PHYTOSAURUS

HERRERASAURUS

COELOPHYSIS

HESPEROSUCHUS

This reptile hunted near rivers and streams in what is now the southwestern United States.

HORSETAIL FERNS

28 MYA:
ARLY PTEROSAURS
AKE FLIGHT

210 MYA: FIRST
EARLY MAMMALS
APPEAR

201 MYA: EXTINCTION
EVENT ENDS THE TRIASSIC

220 MYA

210 MYA

200 MYA

DINOSAURS TAKE OVER
Jurassic Period

RHAMPHORHYNCHUS

During the Jurassic, it finally happened: The supercontinent of Pangea fractured into two separate continents, **Laurasia** and **Gondwana**. The climate became warmer and wetter—conditions perfect for lush plant life. With all this food to eat, many kinds of plant-eating dinosaurs thrived. Some of them grew to enormous sizes, like the long-necked **sauropods**. Predators capable of attacking these giants also appeared during the Jurassic. One of the mightiest was *Allosaurus*, a hunter with eight-inch (20-cm)-long claws and dozens of tearing teeth.

DIPLODOCUS

APATOSAURUS

Reaching New Heights

Sauropods such as *Diplodocus* and *Apatosaurus* were some of the mightiest plant eaters that have ever lived on Earth. They used their extremely long necks to **browse** on leaves from the tops of trees or to mow down **vegetation** without having to move their massive bodies.

AVIAN DINOSAUR
AY-vee-un-DYE-noh-sor
(noun) any of a group of theropod dinosaurs that survived the Cretaceous mass extinction event and are known today as birds

SAUROPOD
SOR-uh-pahd
(noun) any of a group of plant-eating dinosaurs that mostly walked on four legs and had long necks and tails and small heads

201–145 MYA

JURASSIC TIMELINE*

The 56-million-year Jurassic Period saw lots of new animals and a changing landscape:

*All dates are approximate

190 MYA: FIRST FROGS EVOLVE

180 MYA: FIRST MODERN OCEAN BEGINS TO FORM

200 MYA: EARLY BUTTERFLIES AND MOTHS EVOLVE

200 MYA

190 MYA

180 MYA

Flocks of Feathers

During the Jurassic Period, some smaller theropod dinosaurs developed feathers and began to use their forelimbs to take flight. This group of flying dinosaurs, or **avian dinosaurs**, would go on to survive the extinction of the rest of the dinosaurs. Today, we call them birds.

ARCHAEOPTERYX

CAMPTOSAURUS

MONKEY PUZZLE TREE

ALLOSAURUS

STEGOSAURUS

Shrinking Insects

Before birds evolved, enormous insects ruled the skies. The largest dragonfly had a **wingspan** the same size as a hawk's today! However, during the Jurassic, birds began to take flight and prey on this banquet of bugs. Smaller, more nimble insects evolved that could evade these flying predators.

GLYPTOPS

168 MYA: FIRST-KNOWN STEGOSAURS APPEAR

161 MYA: FEATHERED DINOSAURS EMERGE

145 MYA: END OF THE JURASSIC PERIOD

170 MYA   160 MYA   150 MYA

WHEN DINOSAURS RULED
Cretaceous Period

It was a good time to be a dinosaur. In the Cretaceous, the planet's land separated into more distinct continents and different dinosaurs reigned on each. History's most iconic species lived during this time period. **Titanosaurs** as big as jumbo jets stomped their way across South America and Africa. In Asia, *Velociraptor* sprinted on swift legs. And North America was terrorized by one of the biggest, mightiest land predators that ever lived: *Tyrannosaurus rex.*

PARASAUROLOPHUS

MAGNOLIA

ANGIOSPERM
AN-jee-uh-sperm
(noun) a flowering plant

TITANOSAUR
tye-TAN-uh-sor
(noun) any of a group of approximately 40 species of sauropod dinosaurs, some of which were the largest animals ever known to walk the planet

In Bloom
The first flowering plants, or **angiosperms**, appeared in the early Cretaceous. They would provide a food source for more than a million species of insects, including **pollinators** such as bees and butterflies.

CONIOPHIS

145–66 MYA

CRETACEOUS TIMELINE*
The Cretaceous Period lasted 79 million years and ended the reign of the dinosaurs:

*All dates are approximate

140 MYA: FIRST FLOWERING PLANTS APPEAR

130 MYA: EARLY BEES EMERGE

128 MYA: FIRST SNAKES APPEAR

140 MYA	130 MYA	120 MYA	110 MY

Dinosaur Superstar

Tyrannosaurus rex is history's most famous dinosaur for a reason. It was the size of a bus, with 60 banana-sized teeth and jaws so big they could have fit a full-grown human inside. This hunter stomped across the Cretaceous landscape for millions of years.

STEGOCERAS

TRICERATOPS

TYRANNOSAURUS

Small and Furry

Lush Cretaceous forests were home not only to dinosaurs, but also to early **mammals** that scurried at their feet. The behavior of these small creatures was diverse. There were gliders, swimmers, burrowers, climbers, and more.

ALPHADON

66 MYA: EXTINCTION EVENT, ENDS THE MESOZOIC ERA

68–66 MYA: WHEN *TYRANNOSAURUS REX* LIVED

100 MYA: TOOTHY SEABIRDS TAKE FLIGHT

100 MYA   90 MYA   80 MYA   70 MYA

STRONG SKELETONS
Amazing Dinosaur Anatomy

To learn about what dinosaurs were like, paleontologists start with their bones! Even though finding a complete skeleton is rare, just one fossilized bone can tell scientists a lot about what a dinosaur looked like, how it lived, and much more.

ANATOMY

uh-NAT-uh-mee

(noun) the structural makeup of the body and parts of a living thing

VERTEBRATE

VER-tuh-brut

(noun) an animal with a backbone

CAUDAL VERTEBRAE (TAIL BONES)

SPINE

SCAPULA (SHOULDER BLADE)

CORACOID (SHOULDER BONE)

ILLIUM (HIP BONE)

HIPS

FEMUR (THIGH BONE)

METATARSALS (FOOT BONES)

RIBS

STERNUM (BREASTBONE)

TIBIA AND FIBULA (SHIN BONES)

PHALANGES (TOE BONES)

ALL IN THE HIPS

Scientists divide dinosaurs into two main groups, the **saurischians** (*sor-IH-skee-unz*) and **ornithischians** (*or-nuh-THIH-skee-unz*). The most important difference is in the arrangement of their hip bones. The saurischians—which includes theropods such as *T. rex* and sauropods such as *Diplodocus*—had hips arranged more like those of lizards. The ornithischians—such as *Stegosaurus* and *Triceratops*—had hip bones positioned more like those of birds.

BONUS BONES

Some dinosaurs, including *Allosaurus* and *T. rex*, had an extra set of riblike bones that stretched across their belly. *T. rex* had around 60 of these bones, called **gastralia** (*gass-TRAY-lee-uh*). Experts think these belly bones would have helped huge dinosaurs push air in and out of their lungs.

ON THE MOVE

The shape of a dinosaur's skeleton can tell scientists how it moved. The earliest dinosaurs were all **bipeds** that walked on two legs. Later, some dinosaurs became **quadrupeds** that walked on all four legs. Details of a dinosaur's skeleton tell which type of mover it was. For example, bipeds had front limbs with slimmer bones than quadrupeds.

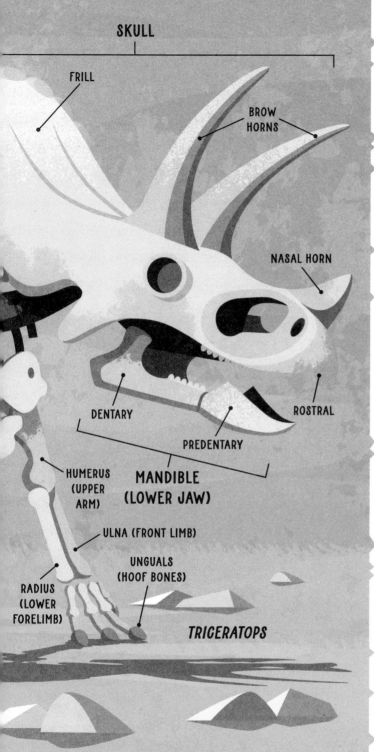

SKULL

FRILL

BROW
HORNS

NASAL HORN

DENTARY

PREDENTARY

ROSTRAL

HUMERUS
(UPPER
ARM)

MANDIBLE
(LOWER JAW)

ULNA (FRONT LIMB)

UNGUALS
(HOOF BONES)

RADIUS
(LOWER
FORELIMB)

TRICERATOPS

READING RINGS

Many animals—including dinosaurs—have bones that grow in layers. Scientists can cut into a dinosaur bone to see **growth rings** that look like the rings of a tree. They can count the rings to see how old a dinosaur was when it died. Experts have learned that *T. rex* went through a major growth spurt during its teenage years—just like humans do!

INSIDE A BONE

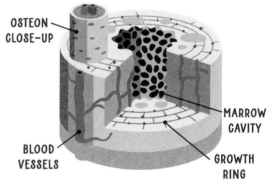

OSTEON
CLOSE-UP

BLOOD
VESSELS

MARROW
CAVITY

GROWTH
RING

A *FRILLING* TRANSFORMATION

The brow horns of *Triceratops* changed over its lifetime from backward-facing to forward-facing. Scientists believe these changes could have indicated how old the dinosaur was. Other dinosaurs also had features that changed over time. For instance, as a *Protoceratops* grew up, its frill got much larger, showing off the dinosaur's health and strength. That feature may have helped it attract a mate.

PERFECT PROTECTION

Skeletons provided protection inside and out. Some bones, like the rib cage, kept a dinosaur's heart and lungs safe inside its body. Other bones, like the enormous **frill** of a *Triceratops*, protected the dinosaur's vulnerable neck from attack.

TRICERATOPS

HEAD TO TAIL
Brilliant Bodies

When they're in the ground, fossils don't look like much more than brown or black rocks. But scientists can use fossil evidence to recreate dinosaurs in living detail, learning everything from their colors, to the ways they used their tails, to even the sounds they made.

COLORFUL CREATURES

For a long time, paleontologists could only guess at what color the dinosaurs might have been. But recently, high-powered microscopes have allowed scientists to see that some fossilized feathers and scales contain tiny, **pigment**-filled sacs called **melanosomes**. They show that dinosaurs came in a whole range of colors. For example, feathered *Anchiornis* had black-and-white striped wings and a red mohawk, while armored *Borealopelta* was rust-colored on top, with a pale underside.

FANTASTIC FEATHERS

Fossilized feathers are incredibly rare. Although scientists know that all dinosaurs sported scales, recent discoveries show some species were also feathered. Experts often debate about which species featured feathers. While many smaller dinosaurs of the Cretaceous were likely feathered, the largest dinosaurs probably were not. That's because a fluffy covering of feathers could have made their big bodies hold in too much heat. There was at least one exception, however: *Yutyrannus* was a 30-foot (9-m) feathered tyrannosaur! It had long, fuzzy feathers called **filaments**, similar to those of a baby chick.

FILAMENTS

YUTYRANNUS

TALL TAIL

The cracking sound a whip makes happens when the tip travels faster than the speed of sound, making a noise called a **sonic boom**. And some scientists think *Apatosaurus*, a giant, plant-eating dinosaur might have created the same effect with its 40-foot (12-m) whiplike tail. Other experts disagree, but they say it's possible that *Apatosaurus* swung its tail around to fend off attackers.

APATOSAURUS

ANCHIORNIS

FILAMENT

FILL-uh-muhnt

(noun) a fuzzy structure that covered some dinosaurs and that eventually evolved into feathers

MELANOSOME

muh-LAN-uh-sohm

(noun) a small, pigment-filled sac inside of cells that gives some body parts their color

STANDING UP

Dinosaurs weren't just big lizards or land-dwelling crocodiles. One thing that made them different from these scaly cousins was their upright stance. Unlike a lizard or crocodile, who holds its limbs out to the side of its body (a posture called **sprawling**), a dinosaur's limbs were positioned straight under its body. That allowed them to use less energy to move around faster.

SPRAWLING POSTURE

UPRIGHT POSTURE

HANDY HEADGEAR

Many dinosaur species sported striking head accessories such as horns and frills. But the most unusual of all may have been *Parasaurolophus*. This dinosaur had a **crest** that stretched three feet (1m) behind its head! And it wasn't just for show. Airways ran through the crest and connected it to the dinosaur's nose. *Parasaurolophus* would have used its horn like a trumpet, probably to communicate with others of its kind. Scientists think different species may have sounded off in different notes.

CREST

PARASAUROLOPHUS

ON THE MENU
Dining Like a Dinosaur

How do you figure out the favorite foods of animals that have been dead for 100 million years? By examining their teeth, stomachs, and even their poop!

Sometimes, paleontologists are lucky enough to discover a dinosaur fossil with **cololites** (*KAH-luh-lytes*), or the preserved contents of its stomach. Other times, paleontologists find fossilized dinosaur dung, called **coprolites**. These finds are incredibly rare because both stomach contents and dinosaur dung are generally made up of soft material that doesn't fossilize well. Mostly, experts use dinosaur teeth to get an idea of what a particular species ate.

CARNIVORE
KAHR-nuh-vor
(noun) an animal that feeds mostly on other animals

COPROLITE
KAH-pruh-lyte
(noun) fossilized dung

GASTROLITH
GASS-truh-lith
(noun) a stone eaten by an animal in order to grind up and help digest food

HERBIVORE
HER-buh-vor
(noun) an animal that feeds mostly on plants

OMNIVORE
AHM-nuh-vor
(noun) an animal that feeds on both animals and plants

GIGANOTOSAUR

TROODON

MEAT EATERS

Meat-eating dinosaurs, the **carnivores**, had teeth adapted for cutting and tearing flesh. Some, such as *Troodon*, had many curved, short **serrated** teeth that looked similar to small steak knives and were perfect for shearing off chunks of meat.

PEGLIKE TEETH

IGUANODON

PLANT EATERS

Most dinosaur species—about 65 percent—were **herbivores**, or plant eaters. They grazed on a wide range of plants, from tough conifers and cycads to tender ferns and mosses. Starting in the Cretaceous, some may have even snacked on newly evolving flowering plants. The teeth of herbivorous dinosaurs were as varied as their diets. Some, such as *Iguanodon*, chewed up their food with flat teeth good for grinding.

SLICING TEETH

CONE-SHAPED TEETH

SERRATED TEETH

SPINOSAURUS

OMNIVOROUS EATERS

Some dinosaurs ate both meat and plants. Scientists have so far discovered about 30 species of these **omnivores**. One was *Deinocheirus*, a dinosaur so odd-looking that scientists have described it as a "duck-billed ostrich camel." This toothless, humpbacked, feathered animal was taller than an elephant. It snacked on both plants and fish in what is now Mongolia. Experts think it could have been the biggest omnivorous dinosaur of all time.

Others, such as *Giganotosaurus*, had long, strong serrated teeth that were good at slicing through large pieces of their meal. And fish-eating predators such as *Spinosaurus* had teeth shaped like cones (similar to those of modern crocodiles), which were great at piercing the slippery skin of fish.

Since *Deinocheirus* had no teeth, scientists think it used gastroliths to help it digest the soft foods it ate.

DIPLODOCUS

FLAT TEETH

STOMACH WITH GASTROLITHS

Others didn't chew at all. Some long-necked sauropods used their spoon-shaped teeth to strip leaves from plants, while others such as *Diplodocus*, used their peglike teeth to rake leaves off of trees. Because they didn't chew, these dinosaurs needed another way to break down their meals. So they swallowed stones, called **gastroliths**, that would grind up the food in their guts. Many modern birds do the same.

BABY DINOSAURS
Family Life

CITIPATI

About 75 million years ago, a sudden sandstorm or mudslide caught a dinosaur parent by surprise. The dinosaur was frozen in time, fossilized while sitting on top of a nest of eggs with its wings spread wide, seemingly protecting its unhatched young. The fossil, belonging to a species called *Citipati*, confirmed scientists' theory that some dinosaurs nested, just as modern birds do.

BROOD
BROOD
(verb) to sit on or incubate eggs

CLUTCH
KLUTCH
(noun) a group of eggs laid all at once

EMBRYO
EM-bree-oh
(noun) an animal in its earliest stages of growth developing inside an egg or its mother's body

CLUTCH OF EGGS LAID IN A RING

BIG AND BIRDLIKE

It's tough to imagine a creature that weighs as much as a rhinoceros delicately **brooding** its eggs. But the biggest dinosaurs might have done just that. Scientists think that bigger species arranged their **clutch** in a circle around the edge of their nests, then sat in the middle. That way the adult dinosaur could protect its eggs without crushing them and also keep them warm.

TEAMWORK

Some dinosaurs didn't just brood their eggs. They also cared for their little ones once they hatched. "Egg Mountain" is a fossil **site** in Montana where paleontologists discovered multiple nests belonging to the dinosaur *Maiasaura* grouped together. Egg, baby, and adult dinosaur fossils have also been discovered at Egg Mountain, evidence that some dinosaurs tended to their young.

WINGS COVER THE NEST
IN A BROODING POSITION

MOUND-SHAPED NEST

HANDS OFF

Not all dinosaurs were such caring parents. Instead of brooding their eggs, some dinosaurs laid them and left them behind. Some species buried their eggs inside mounds made of soil or plants, which helped protect and keep them warm. Others dug holes in the ground for their eggs, like turtles do.

ANATOMY OF AN EGG

Some early dinosaur eggs were soft and leathery, like turtles' eggs. But later, most dinosaurs laid hard-shelled eggs, as modern birds do. Also like birds' eggs, dinosaur eggs came in a wide range of colors, from blue-green to red speckled. A dinosaur egg sheltered the growing **embryo** and held all the nutrition it would need before it hatched.

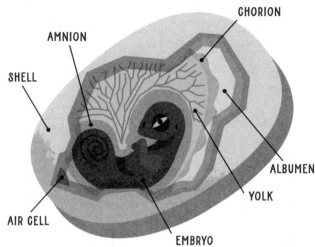

CHORION

AMNION

SHELL

ALBUMEN

YOLK

AIR CELL

EMBRYO

Shell: The hard shell was covered with thousands of tiny holes called **pores** that allowed oxygen to pass through so the embryo could breathe. The pores also allowed waste gases and water to exit the egg.

Membranes: Called the **chorion** (*KOR-ee-ahn*) and the **amnion** (*AM-nee-ahn*), these transparent layers prevented **bacteria** (which could make the little dinosaur sick) from entering the egg.

Albumen (*al-BYOO-muhn*): Also called the "white," this outer layer of the egg provided the embryo with **protein** and water and acted as a shock absorber.

Yolk: Full of fat, carbohydrates, vitamins, and minerals, the yolk was the embryo's food source while it developed.

Air Cell: Near the end of development, the baby dinosaur broke into this pocket of air and took its first breaths.

DINOSAUR LIFE
How Dinos Spent Their Days

When they weren't eating or sleeping, what exactly did dinosaurs do? Evidence shows that these ancient animals led complex lives. Some socialized in groups, others sheltered underground, and one species even left the land to hunt in the water!

ICHNITE

UNDERGROUND LAIR

In 2007, paleontologists in Montana made an incredible discovery: the fossils of an adult and two young *Oryctodromeus* dinosaurs inside a **burrow**. They may have used these underground shelters to care for their babies or to escape extreme temperatures. These dinosaurs were plant-eating creatures that had strong arms and shoulders to help them dig their hideaways.

ORYCTODROMEUS BURROW

PADDLE OUT

For a long time, no fossils of *Spinosaurus* were discovered with the tail intact. Experts assumed this dinosaur must have had a long, pointy tail similar to others in its family group. But—surprise!—when a *Spinosaurus* tail was finally found in Morocco in 2020, it resembled a giant paddle. This tail shape, scientists say, could only belong to a semi-**aquatic**, or swimming, dinosaur. Perhaps *Spinosaurus* hunted underwater, like a giant crocodile.

PADDLE-SHAPED TAIL

SPINOSAURUS

GET IN FORMATION

Step in soft ground and you might leave a footprint behind. Dinosaurs sometimes left footprints behind, too. If conditions were just perfect—hot sun to harden the footprint followed by a wash of mud or other material to fill it in—these prints could then turn into fossils. These fossilized footprints, called **ichnites**, have been discovered all over the world. Some show that certain dinosaurs ate, slept, and lived together in groups. Other prints show that some other dinosaurs could have teamed up to hunt in packs like wolves—perhaps including *Tyrannosaurus rex*!

ICHNITE

IK-nyte

(noun) a fossil footprint

NOCTURNAL

nahk-TER-nul

(adjective) active mostly at night

UP ALL NIGHT

When did dinosaurs sleep? Evidence suggests that while some species had waking hours during the day, other species may have been **nocturnal**, or active at night. Scientists compared the ear bones and eye sockets of dinosaur fossils to those of living nocturnal animals and found two species of theropods that likely hunted by moonlight. One dinosaur found in Mongolia, *Shuvuuia deserti*, probably had excellent night vision and hearing, possibly as good as a modern owl's.

SHUVUUIA DESERTI

LONG TRIP

The largest dinosaurs to walk Earth may have **migrated**, or traveled, hundreds of miles. Scientists discovered smooth, rusty pink stones in what is now Wyoming that they think dinosaurs used as gastroliths. Long-necked sauropods may have gulped down these stones in what is now Wisconsin, then walked 600 miles (1,000km) before dying and depositing the stones. These grazing dinosaurs likely made their long journey in search of food, just like plant-eating antelope and wildebeest do today.

ON THE HUNT
Dinosaur Offenses

Some dinosaurs were fearsome. They stalked the Mesozoic landscape with sharp teeth, slashing claws, and keen senses. One of the mightiest **predators** was *Tyrannosaurus rex*. It killed and ate mega-herbivores like *Triceratops*—and almost anything else it came across.

Open Wide

Sixty serrated teeth up to 12 inches (30cm) long were ideal for shearing through flesh. *T. rex* didn't chew its food. Instead, it tore off huge chunks and then swallowed them whole.

PREDATOR

PRED-uh-ter

(noun) an animal that lives mostly by killing and eating other animals

SCAVENGE

SKAV-inj

(verb) to eat already dead or decaying material (such as other animals)

Claw-some

What's up with the tiny arms of a *T. rex*? Some scientists think they were useless **appendages** left over from the dinosaur's earlier relatives. But others think they were weapons that allowed *T. rex* to slash at prey with its four-inch (10-cm) claws.

TRICERATOPS

Big Bite

T. rex had a huge head with a five-foot (1.5-m)-long skull. Its huge, muscular jaw gave it the most powerful bite of any land animal, so strong it could crush a car. This enabled *T. rex* to chomp through the bones of its prey.

Sniffing Skills

How did *T. rex* track down its prey? Scientists think that sometimes *T. rex* chased down live prey and other times it may have **scavenged** dead animals. They do know that *T. rex* had large **olfactory** *(ahl-FAK-tuh-ree)* regions, or portions of its brain dedicated to processing odors—evidence that this predator had a keen sense of smell.

Sharp Sight

This dinosaur had eyeballs the size of apples—the biggest of any land animal in history. Its forward-facing, wide-set eyes would have been excellent at picking prey out of the landscape. And it's likely that *T. rex* could detect **ultraviolet light**, a range of colors not visible to humans. That could have made it skilled at spotting prey in a thick forest.

TYRANNOSAURUS REX

Full Speed Ahead

The powerful legs and tail of a *T. rex* would have helped give this massive predator speed. Experts estimate it could run up to 15 miles an hour (24kph). That's fast for an animal the size of a bus!

MORE MONSTERS OF THE MESOZOIC

While most predatory dinosaurs killed by slashing or chomping, *Majungasaurus* used its short, stout snout to grab prey and hold on until the animal couldn't fight any longer. It's also one of the few dinosaurs known for sure to be a **cannibal**—it ate others of its own species.

MAJUNGASAURUS

Velociraptor was only about the size of a wolf, but this predator more than made up for its small stature with massive, curved **talons** on each of its second toes. These claws would have been ideal for pinning prey down for easy eating. *Velociraptor* kept these talons sharp by keeping them retracted, like those of a cat, and by holding them in the air. This prevented the talons from scraping on the ground and becoming dull.

VELOCIRAPTOR

CLAW HELD UP

POWERFUL PROTECTION
Dinosaur Defenses

DORSAL PLATE

How did the herbivores of the Mesozoic protect themselves? Some deterred attackers by living in groups. Others used their enormous size to make predators back off. Still others had built-in defenses to keep hunters at bay, such as body **armor** and tail weapons.

STEGOSAURUS

OSTEODERM
AH-stee-uh-derm
(noun) a bony plate in the skin of an armored dinosaur

THAGOMIZER
THAG-uh-mye-zer
(noun) the cluster of spikes on the tail of a *Stegosaurus*

ALLOSAURUS

WICKED WEAPON

Any hungry predator that came upon a *Stegosaurus* would have probably thought twice before trying to make a meal out this dinosaur. The strong, powerful tail of a *Stegosaurus* ended in a cluster of spikes. This body part is called a **thagomizer**. A cartoonist invented the name as a joke, but it was so popular with scientists that they adopted the name. There's no doubt the thagomizer was a deadly weapon. Scientists have found *Allosaurus* remains with puncture wounds that exactly match the tail spikes of a *Stegosaurus*.

Though it was a member of a family of armored dinosaurs, *Stegosaurus* probably didn't use the finlike **dorsal** plates that ran along its spine for defense. Instead, experts think one way *Stegosaurus* could have used its plates was to help the animal control its body temperature. A network of blood vessels inside each plate would have run near the surface of the dinosaur's skin, near the air. This allowed the plates to absorb heat from the air or help release extra heat from the dinosaur's body.

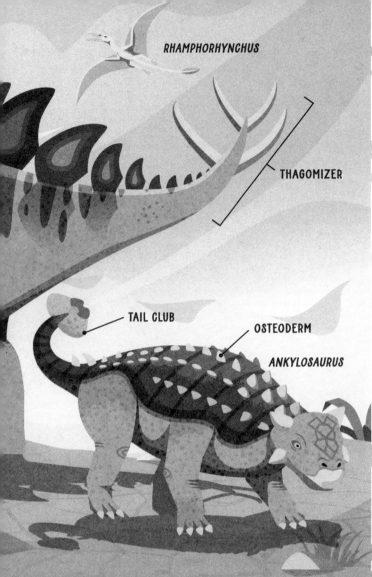

RHAMPHORHYNCHUS

THAGOMIZER

TAIL CLUB

OSTEODERM

ANKYLOSAURUS

EXTREME ARMOR

Ankylosaurus is sometimes called a "living tank." This dinosaur didn't move fast, but it didn't need to. That's because this dinosaur's top and sides were almost completely covered with thick, protective plates of bone called **osteoderms**. Some species even had armored eyelids!

If all that wasn't enough to deter a predator, the long tail of an *Ankylosaurus* was tipped with a nasty club. Made of vertebrae and osteoderms woven together into a hard knob, the tail clubs of some species were even covered in spikes, similar to the thagomizer of a *Stegosaurus*. Scientists aren't yet sure of the purpose of the club, but fossilized **ankylosaurs** with damaged clubs show that it could have been used for fighting. Perhaps, some experts think, *Ankylosaurus* swiped at the ankles of any predator that dared to come too close.

HERD MENTALITY

Paleontologists believe that sauropods may have taken the safety in numbers approach, staying together in **herds**. A lone predator, such as a *T. rex*, would have been outnumbered. Faced with a large group, the hunter may have been less likely to attack.

ALAMOSAURUS HERD

T. REX

HORRIBLE HORNS?

It's easy to imagine a *Triceratops* fending off an attacking *T. rex* with its trio of long, sharp horns. But scientists think some horned dinosaurs, called **ceratopsians** *(sair-uh-TAHP-see-unz),* didn't use their spectacular skull spikes on predators. Instead, they may have used them to impress potential mates and to lock horns with rivals, the way modern animals with antlers, such as elk, do.

TRICERATOPS

TAKING FLIGHT
Dinosaurs in the Sky

The first birds didn't look much like modern ones. They had sharp teeth and claws and long, bony tails. Birds first evolved in the late Jurassic, from a line of meat-eating theropod dinosaurs. This same group included *Tyrannosaurus rex*—meaning that its closest living relatives are birds such as ostriches and chickens! Over millions of years, birds developed beaks and lost their teeth and tails to become the creatures we know today.

PYGOSTYLE
PYE-guh-style

(noun) a plate of bone found in most birds that is formed by fused vertebrae in the tail and used to control flight

TRANSITIONAL FOSSIL
tran-SISH-uh-nul-FAH-sul

(noun) a fossil that shows characteristics of its relatives of one kind that lived before and its relatives of another kind that came after

ARCHAEOPTERYX

This dinosaur had teeth, claws, and a bony tail, like a reptile. But it also had feathers that looked a lot like those of a modern bird! *Archaeopteryx* lived on ancient islands dotted with trees. It could probably fly in short bursts, like a modern quail or pheasant. Its fossil, which shows a clear imprint of feathers, is one of the most famous finds in history. Paleontologists call it a **transitional fossil** that marks the **evolution** of modern birds.

Teardrop-shaped feathers of *Confuciusornis sanctus*

TOOTH

GARGANTUAVIS

Most Mesozoic birds only grew about as big as crows. But not *Gargantuavis philoinos*. This huge, ostrichlike bird lived in the late Cretaceous in what is now France. It stood between six and ten feet (1.8–3m) tall—taller than an adult human. Because of its size, scientists think it was a **flightless** bird, but they are not sure. If it did fly, it would have had to support its big body with a wingspan wider than 13 feet (4m)!

CONFUCIUSORNIS

While *Archaeopteryx* looked like a reptile with wings, crow-sized *Confuciusornis* was much more birdlike. This animal had a toothless beak and is the first known dinosaur to have the last few vertebrae in its tail fused together. Called a **pygostyle**, this bone structure is present in today's birds and helps them steer while flying. Some species of *Confuciusornis* also had two long, teardrop-shaped feathers that grew from the end of its tail. Scientists think that these species may have used their fancy feathers to attract mates.

FALCATAKELY

Scientists were stunned when they realized this Cretaceous-era bird had a unique beak. Its **morphology** (mor-FAH-luh-jee), or appearance, was different from that of other birds experts had discovered living around the same time. The beak of *Falcatakely* looked a bit like a modern toucan's, but the fossil specimen sported a single tooth at the tip. Since birds have delicate, hollow bones that can easily break down, their fossils are rare. Paleontologists have found only one fossilized *Falcatakely* skull so far. But this discovery suggests that the birds that flew overhead during the age of dinosaurs had a variety of features.

RECORD-BREAKERS
Extraordinary Dinosaurs

We're living in a golden age of dinosaur discovery. Paleontologists find a new species an average of once a week! More than 700 dinosaur species have been discovered so far, and experts know that this is just a small fraction of all dinosaurs that ever existed. But of them all, which species stand out?

STRUTHIOMIMUS

BIGGEST: *ARGENTINOSAURUS*

The title for biggest dinosaur is always changing as new, ever more enormous fossils are unearthed. But surely one of the largest land animals ever to shake the Mesozoic was *Argentinosaurus*. Though they have found only a few bones, scientists estimate this titanosaur could have measured as long as a 737 airplane and been heavier than 20 hippos! Despite its massive size, this giant didn't move quickly. It only had a **gait**, or pace, of about five miles an hour (7kph).

CURSORIAL
kur-SOR-ee-uhl
(adjective) adapted to run fast and/ or for long distances

DENTAL BATTERY
DEN-tuhl-BAT-uh-ree
(noun) rows of teeth tightly packed together to form a surface for grinding food

SMALLEST: *MICRORAPTOR*

A few species compete for the title of tiniest dinosaur. One of the smallest of them all was *Microraptor*, weighing about two pounds (0.9kg) and measuring only a foot (31cm) tall. *Microraptor* had feathers on both its front and hind legs, and a cluster on the end of its tail. But it didn't fly. Instead, it would leap from the tops of trees and spread out its limbs wide to glide, like a flying squirrel. Scientists think the feathers of *Microraptor* were **iridescent** (*ih-ruh-DEH-suhnt*), like those of a peacock.

FASTEST: THE ORNITHOMIMIDS

Fossils can't show speed. But scientists can use what they know about the anatomy of fast-moving animals alive today to estimate how speedy ancient species might have been. Some of the fastest dinosaurs ever were the Ornithomimids. With their long legs, long necks, and small heads, they looked similar to ostriches. Ornithomimids were **cursorial** animals, meaning they had bodies adapted for running. They might have been able to reach speeds of up to 50 miles an hour (80kph)—as fast as a sprinting lion.

SMARTEST: *TROODON*

There's no way to give an extinct animal an intelligence test. But when judging smarts, scientists often look to how big a creature's brain is compared to its body size, also called its **brain-to-body ratio**. (Humans, chimpanzees, and dolphins have some of the largest brain-to-body ratios of all living animals.) By that measure, *Troodon* may have been one of the smartest dinosaurs of all. Its big brain powered keen hearing, eyesight, and smell, which this hunter used to sneak up on prey. *Troodon* were also protective parents, with the males in charge of brooding the eggs.

TROODON

TOOTHIEST: *NIGERSAURUS*

A large dinosaur with hundreds of teeth might sound terrifying. But *Nigersaurus* was an herbivore nicknamed the "Mesozoic cow." This dinosaur had an odd-shaped face with a wide, flat mouth that some scientists have compared to a vacuum cleaner. *Nigersaurus* had what's called a **dental battery**: multiple rows of teeth tightly packed together to form a surface for grinding food. The top and bottom of this dinosaur's mouth each held a row of about 50 flat-edged teeth. But underneath were about 500 more teeth waiting in the wings. As the front teeth wore out, new ones would move in to take their place. Scientists think *Nigersaurus* may have needed to replace each tooth after just two weeks. That's a lot of chewing!

DINOSAUR NEIGHBORS
What Lived Alongside the Dinosaurs?

Dinosaurs may have ruled the land during the Mesozoic, but that doesn't mean they were the only creatures around. Far from it! All kinds of animals lived alongside the dinosaurs, scurrying under their feet, swimming through the seas, and soaring overhead.

Flying High

Scientists have discovered more than 150 species of **pterosaurs**. They are commonly mistaken for flying dinosaurs, but pterosaurs were cousins of dinosaurs that belonged to a separate order of reptiles. Besides insects, they were the first animals ever to fly.

MOSASAUR

MOH-zuh-sor

(noun) any of a group of large carnivorous marine lizards with limbs shaped like paddles that lived during the Cretaceous Period

PLESIOSAUR

PLEE-see-uh-sor

(noun) any of a group of carnivorous aquatic reptiles with long necks, small heads, short tails, wide bodies, and flippers that lived from the late Triassic into the late Cretaceous Periods

PTEROSAUR

TAIR-uh-sor

(noun) any of a group of flying reptiles with featherless wings in the form of a thin skin that ran from the side of its body, along its arm, and ended at its long fingerlike digit

PLESIOSAURS

Plesiosaurs swam through the oceans using their four enormous flippers and feasted on fish and other **marine** animals. Some could be almost 50 feet (15m) long! They used their long necks to slither their small heads up close to prey without being noticed. Then—*CHOMP*!

MOSASAURS

The Cretaceous ocean's top prehistoric predators were the **mosasaurs**. The deadliest of them all was *Tylosaurus*, which used its muscular tail and its webbed, paddlelike limbs to power through the water. Prey were no match for the huge toothy jaws of *Tylosaurus*, which it used to swallow its meal whole.

ARCHELON

The largest turtle ever to live, it could grow as big as a small car.

TYLOSAURUS

PTERANODON

QUETZALCOATLUS
The largest flying animal to ever live, this pterosaur was the size of a small airplane!

ICHTHYOSAURS
These ancient reptilian ocean-dwellers resembled modern-day dolphins and fish. They were swift swimmers, perhaps topping 25 miles an hour (40kph).

ICHTHYOSAURUS

PLESIOSAURUS

Scaly Survivors
Around the time the first dinosaurs evolved, so did the first **crocodilians**. By the late Cretaceous, this group had short legs, armored scales, and an aquatic lifestyle. Crocodiles haven't changed much in the millions of years since—even after surviving the Cretaceous asteroid impact and two **ice ages**!

Mammals Move In
Mammals would rise up to dominate Earth after the extinction event nearly 66 million years ago that killed nearly all the dinosaurs. The earliest mammals were small: The biggest of them were no larger than house cats. After the **non-avian dinosaurs** were wiped out, new **habitats** and environments would become available and mammals would move in. Eventually, they evolved into everything from tiny mice to enormous elephants… and us.

CASTOROCAUDA

SARCOSUCHUS IMPERATOR
Nicknamed SuperCroc, this was one of the biggest crocodiles that ever lived. It measured about 40 feet (12m) long and weighed about 9 tons (8t). It dominated the rivers of what is now the Sahara Desert, ambushing any animals that entered its watery home.

GOING EXTINCT
The End of the Age of Dinosaurs

Dinosaurs walked Earth for over 175 million years. That's about 500 times as long as modern humans have been around! Dinosaurs lived on every corner of the planet, ate everything from ferns to insects to one another, and grew to enormous sizes the likes of which land animals have never reached again. They were one of the most successful animal groups to ever exist. But about 66 million years ago, something happened to end the reign of the dinosaurs.

THE BEGINNING OF THE END

It all started when a giant **asteroid** came zooming out of space and slammed into Earth. The impact threw a huge amount of rock and dirt into the air. In addition to the devastation at the site itself, effects from the crash landing would be felt across the planet. There were massive **tsunamis** (soo-NAH-meez) and wildfires. Volcanoes erupted and gale-force winds blasted. **Acid rain** fell. Dust filled the sky, blocking sunlight and causing plants to shrivel and die. Over time, temperatures rose and runaway **global warming** roasted the planet. The aftereffects of the impact lasted for centuries.

ALAMOSAURUS

PACHYCEPHALOSAURUS

WHO SURVIVED?

In total, about three in every four species on Earth died out. Nearly all the dinosaurs were among the victims. But some animals made it through. They were creatures that could take shelter by burrowing underground, diving underwater, or flying. Some animals stayed alive by eating dead plants and fungi. Others survived by eating **carrion**, such as the carcasses of dinosaurs and other animals. Some of these scrappy survivors were mammals, and it was about to be their turn to rule the planet.

ASTEROID

AST-uh-royd

(noun) any of thousands of rocky objects in space that move in orbits and have diameters from a fraction of a mile to nearly 600 miles (1,000km)

IMPACT CRATER

IM-pakt-KRAY-ter

(noun) a large depression in a planet or moon formed by a fast-traveling object from space striking the ground with great force

QUETZALCOATLUS

TYRANNOSAURUS

STRIKE ZONE

A planet doesn't get hit by a space rock six miles (10km) across and not show the damage. Scientists knew an asteroid that size would leave an **impact crater** more than 63 miles (100km) across. And after years of searching, they finally found it buried below Earth's surface on the coast of Mexico's Yucatán Peninsula. At the crater site, scientists have found **iridium** *(ih-RID-ee-um)* dust, a chemical element common in asteroids but rare on Earth. Scientists also discovered this dust in rock layers all over the planet. These layers also happen to be 66 million years old—the same time the non-avian dinosaurs died. This is solid evidence that the asteroid impact and its aftereffects ended life for most dinosaurs.

UNITED STATES

YUCATÁN PENINSULA

MEXICO

CUBA

Close-up of Mexico's Yucatán Peninsula and the site of the impact crater at Chicxulub

IMPACT SITE

CHICXULUB

YUCATÁN PENINSULA

FROM BONE TO STONE
Fossil Formation

A dinosaur is caught unaware by a sudden mudslide and buried instantly. Millions of years later, a lucky paleontologist carefully removes it from the ground. Its bones are now turned to stone! Fossils show us evidence of dinosaurs and other living things that shared our planet long ago. But how does a living, breathing animal become a fossil?

When a creature dies, its body **decomposes**, or is broken down by tiny **microbes**. Skin, organs, and other **soft tissues** decompose quickly. Hard tissues such as bones and teeth take longer. But most dead things eventually rot away until there is nothing left. In order for an animal to become a fossil, it has to be quickly buried under something like sand, mud, or even ash from an erupting volcano. When that happens, the microbes that do the decomposing can't get the **oxygen** they need to work.

The most common way for a dinosaur to become a fossil is called **petrification**. Over time, layers of **sediment**, such as sand, ash, or mud, build up on top of the dead animal. Each new layer puts more weight on the layers below. Eventually, all this pressure squeezes the sediment around the bones into rock, a geologic process called **lithification** *(lith-uh-fa-KAY-shun)*. During this time, water also slowly moves in and out of the dead dinosaur's bones. As it exits, the water leaves behind **minerals**. These minerals fill the spaces in and around the bone, turning them to stone. Eventually, the bone itself can completely turn to stone, too.

It's very rare for the exact right set of circumstances to happen to form a fossil. Scientists estimate that only one bone in a billion becomes a fossil. Then, a person has to be in just the right place at the right time to make the discovery. It's no wonder a new fossil find is so exciting!

Fossils are as old as the rock layers that surround them.

Most of the dinosaur fossils scientists have discovered come from animals that lived near water.

PETRIFICATION

peh-truh-fuh-KAY-shun

(noun) the conversion of plant or animal matter into stone or something similar to stone

STRATA

STRAY-tuh

(noun) layers of rock

DATING DINOSAURS

Figuring out how old a dinosaur fossil is can tell scientists when the creature lived, what other species it shared the landscape with, and even what was around for it to eat. Sometimes, scientists use **relative dating** to estimate the age of a fossil. Fossils are found in layers of rock, called **strata**, that are laid down one on top of the next through time. The oldest layers are generally buried deeper than the newer layers. By counting and comparing strata, experts can get an idea of how long ago the dinosaur died.

Other times, the surrounding rock layer that holds a fossil will also contain tiny crystals that formed from erupting volcanoes. These crystals are made of special **atoms** that are **radioactive**. These atoms break apart, or **decay**, at a specific rate. By comparing the number of atoms from the original material to the decayed ones, scientists can determine how much time has passed since the rock layer was formed. This way of dating sediment is called **absolute dating**. Scientists can combine both methods to work out a fossil's age.

Radioactive atoms in rocks decay as time goes on. This helps scientists calculate the age of the rock that surrounds a fossil.

RADIOACTIVITY

TIME

AMAZING EVIDENCE
Fabulous Fossil Types

A titanosaur leg bone taller than a professional basketball player. The toothy jawbone of a *Spinosaurus*. A plate that once decorated the back of a *Stegosaurus*. These fossil bones and teeth are called **body fossils**, and they're the most commonly discovered kind of dinosaur remains. But rarely, paleontologists are lucky enough to find **trace fossils**, or evidence of something a dinosaur made, such as nests, footprints, or even poop!

COPROLITE

BONE FRAGMENTS

WALK THIS WAY
Sometimes, paleontologists find trails of fossilized dinosaur ichnites, called **trackways**. Trackways allow scientists to recreate a dinosaur's movements. They can show how long a dinosaur's stride was and sometimes how fast the dinosaur was moving! Scientists have found trackways in what seem like strange places, such as on the ceiling of a cave or on the side of a cliff. But dinosaurs likely weren't walking upside down or cliff climbing. Instead, the ground shifted and changed over the millions of years after the dinosaur strolled by.

BOREALOPELTA
FOSSIL

SLEEPING DRAGON
One day, workers on a mining site dug up something unexpected. It turned out to be a fossilized dinosaur so well-preserved that it looked more like an animal taking a nap than one that had been dead for 110 million years. This **nodosaur**, a relative of *Ankylosaurus* named *Borealopelta*, was so perfectly preserved that it was nicknamed "the Sleeping Dragon." Scientists were able to study individual scales on its armored body and even identify the fossilized contents of its stomach!

WASTE NOT

Rock-hard dinosaur droppings might not sound like the most exciting fossil find. But to scientists, coprolites, or fossilized poop, can be a treasure trove of information. Experts look to this dinosaur dung to see what a dinosaur ate, but also to find evidence of other creatures that shared the same **ecosystem**, or habitat. Coprolites can also reveal other secrets. One *T. rex* coprolite discovered in Canada was jaw-dropping in size, measuring nearly a foot and a half (45cm) long. It was packed with broken bone fragments from a young dinosaur that the *T. rex* had eaten. That provided more evidence that *T. rex*'s jaws were indeed strong enough to crunch through bone.

FOSSIL FEATHERS

Keratin *(KAIR-uh-tin)* is the substance that makes up a rhino's horn, your fingernails, and feathers—even dinosaur feathers. Scientists analyzed the keratin inside fossilized feathers from five dinosaur species discovered in China and Mongolia that lived between 160 and 75 million years ago. They found that the type of keratin that made up the feathers changed over time, becoming gradually lighter and more flexible. While the first feathered dinosaurs used their plumage for keeping warm and to communicate, later, more flexible feathers allowed dinosaurs to take flight.

ARCHAEOPTERYX

BODY FOSSIL

BAH-dee-FAH-sul

(noun) a fossil of bones or teeth that is the most commonly found kind of dinosaur remains

TRACE FOSSIL

TRAYSS-FAH-sul

(noun) a fossil (such as of nests, trails, footprints, dung, or resting marks) that shows evidence of an organism's activities but is not formed from the organism itself

TRAPPED IN TIME

Scientists have found a lot of ancient insects encased in **amber**, or fossilized tree **resin**. But until recently, they had never found dinosaur remains. That changed when the tail of a 99-million-year-old dinosaur was discovered in Myanmar. The 1.4-inch (3.5-cm) chunk of amber contains bones, skin, and feathers from the tail. It's so perfectly preserved that scientists can determine its color: chestnut brown on top and white underneath. They think it belonged to a type of theropod known as a **coelurosaur** *(suh-LOOR-uh-sor)*, a group of dinosaurs with characteristics very similar to birds.

IN THE FIELD
Unearthing the Past

You're covered in dirt, and your back is tired from holding your body in a hunched-over position. But you're totally absorbed in your work as you use a brush to slowly sweep dirt away from a delicate dinosaur fossil. This is how you might feel if you were a paleontologist on a dig. Sometimes, fossils are discovered by accident, such as when a hiker comes across a bone peeking out of the ground or when a construction crew digs up something they weren't expecting. But many times, people find fossils by searching for them. And when someone stumbles across an important find, scientists use all kinds of methods and tools to help them dig up these prehistoric treasures.

EXCAVATE
EK-skuh-vayt
(verb) to dig out and remove

PROSPECT
PRAH-spekt
(verb) to explore an area for fossils and mineral deposits

Step 1: Look for Clues

To unearth new fossils, paleontologists must first know where to dig. Often, they use a geological map of an area that shows how old the rocks in a particular place are. That helps them search for animals that lived during a certain time period. A team of scientists will often split up to walk across an area, looking for small pieces of fossils on the ground. This is called **prospecting**.

Step 2: Dig It Out

Once a fossil is found, the hard work begins. Paleontologists use many different tools to help them **excavate**, or dig out, a fossil. If the fossil is buried underneath a lot of hard rock, they might use a jackhammer or even a bulldozer to remove the **overburden**, or rock layer above the fossil. Next, they might use pickaxes, rock hammers, and chisels to chip away by hand at the **matrix**, or rock immediately surrounding the fossil.

PICKAXE

CHISEL

ROCK HAMMER

Step 3: Make a Map

Once the team has uncovered enough of the fossil find to figure out its outline, they put a special grid over the discovery. Then, they draw the fossils on grid paper, noting the location of every bone that they can see. Later, back in the lab, this map will help the paleontologists identify the exact positions of all the bones. That helps them figure out which bones belonged to which dinosaur.

FIRE-BREATHING FOSSILS?

People in many ancient cultures told tales of enormous dragons with scaly skin and sharp teeth. What inspired so many similar stories in so many different places? Some experts think that when ancient peoples discovered dinosaur fossils, they had no way of knowing the bones belonged to long-dead animals. Instead, they thought they shared the planet with strange creatures, like dragons, cyclopes, and unicorns. Dinosaurs whose fossils looked especially like mythical dragons have been found in what is now Asia and North America—two places with legends of dragons and horned serpents.

Step 4: Keep It Together

It's time to move the fossil for further study. First, the team digs a trench around the fossil. Then, they cover the specimen with a layer of protective paper towels topped with bandages made of burlap dipped in **plaster**. This is called a **field jacket**, and it's just like a cast that a doctor puts around a broken arm. The field jacket keeps the bones and rock from falling apart. Once it hardens, the team removes the fossil from the ground and packs it up. Next stop: the lab!

Dracorex hogwartsia, which means the "Dragon King of Hogwarts," is named after the fictional castle in *Harry Potter*. Its dragonlike horns and knobby facial features may have inspired some ancient myths and stories.

A paleontologist covers a fossil in a field jacket.

PLASTER

BURLAP ROLL

PROTECTIVE TOWELS

IN THE LAB
Fossils Under Study

Once packed for the journey, fossil **specimens** can become so heavy that humans need help from machinery to move them safely. Sometimes, even that doesn't work: One ankylosaur encased in a 20-ton (18-t) rock was so heavy that the forklift moving it sank into the parking lot! Once scientists get the fossil inside the lab, their real work begins.

PREPARATOR

STEREO MICROSCOPE

DUST COLLECTION ARM

AIR SCRIBE

FLAT BLADE CHISEL

HAMMER

ACID BATH

COMPUTED TOMOGRAPHY
kum-PYOO-tud-toh-MAH-gruh-fee
(noun) a process in which a three-dimensional (3-D) image of a body part or fossil is constructed by a computer

SPECIMEN
SPESS-uh-mun
(noun) a portion or quantity of material used by scientists for testing, examination, or study

TOOLS OF THE TRADE

Removing a fossil from the rock that surrounds it is delicate, tricky work. If a fossil is encased in certain types of solid rock, **preparators** may put it inside a vat of **acid** solution to dissolve the rock and leave the fossil unharmed. After a few days in its acid bath, the fossil is ready for the next step: removing any rock that's left. Experts often use picks and small drills that have been altered for this type of work. When the fossil is freed from the rock, preparators assemble it using special **adhesives**, and then brush it with a clear coating to protect the bone from air, moisture, or anything else that could damage it.

CT SCANNER

CAMERA

Paleontologists can use CT scanners to get an inside look at a dinosaur fossil.

SPECIMENS

SPECIMEN

CALIPERS

SCALE BAR

BRUSH

MAGNIFYING LIGHT

UNDER THE SURFACE

Paleontologists use powerful **computed tomography (CT)** scanning technology to get an up-close look at fossils. With CT scanning, they can not only study small details, such as the structure of fossils, but they can even look inside the bones and any fossilized feathers. That's because CT scans work by taking a series of hundreds of X-ray images and using a computer to combine them into a 3-D model. Paleontologists can digitally rotate the fossil and zoom in and out to study every detail.

GETTING SMALL

In the movie *Jurassic Park*, scientists extract dinosaur **DNA** from the blood inside a fossilized mosquito preserved in amber. Since DNA breaks down over time, scientists say it would be nearly impossible to find any piece of DNA complete enough to bring dinosaurs back to life. But scientists really do search for bits of ancient DNA, along with other very small parts of living things, in a field called **molecular paleontology**. Paleontologists can use the information they gather from fossils to solve all kinds of mysteries about how dinosaurs lived, such as what they ate and how closely they were related to modern animals.

IN THE MUSEUM
The Past on Display

Want to walk the length of a sauropod or stand underneath the gaping jaws of a *T. rex*? You don't have to travel back in time—just head to the nearest natural history museum. The American Museum of Natural History in New York City has about 100 dinosaurs on display. But that's just a small portion of its dinosaur collection, which is the largest in the world. That's because museums aren't just a place for regular people to see fossils. They're a place for paleontologists to study them, too.

ARMATURE
AHR-muh-cher
(noun) a framework used by a museum to support a modeled figure or fossil

CAST
KAST
(noun) a reproduction of the shape of an organism's remains

Standing Tall

Decades ago, museums used to drill holes in fossils in order to bolt them directly to metal **armatures**, or mounts. But that caused damage to priceless specimens, destroying parts before modern scientists could study them. Now, armatures are constructed to surround fossil bones and hold them up from the outside. Armatures make it possible to mount some impressively large fossils: The tallest mounted dinosaur in the world is a *Brachiosaurus* that stands in the Natural History Museum in Berlin, Germany. Its bones are 65 percent original fossils!

Fossil or Fake?

"Dippy" the *Diplodocus* is one of the most famous dinosaurs of London's Natural History Museum. But it's not a real fossil: It's a copy, or cast! **Casts** are usually made of lightweight **fiberglass** resin, making them much easier to mount than heavy fossils. Sometimes, casts just fill in the gaps where bones are missing. Other times, entire dinosaurs on display are made of casts. That helps make sure there are enough *T. rex* and *Stegosaurus* replicas to go around to any museum that wants to display one. And it means the real fossils can remain in collections where scientists can use them for study.

DIPLODOCUS

KENTROSAURUS

ARMATURE CLOSE-UP

ARMATURE

SUSPENSION WIRES

QUETZALCOATLUS

A Library of Dinosaurs

Once fossils are prepared in the lab, they are packed in specially made boxes called **cradles**, which have space inside to fit and protect the specimen. Then, they are numbered and the number is recorded in a **catalog**. Some museums organize fossils by where they appear in the dinosaur family tree; others might use the fossils' age or the location where they were discovered.

Hidden World

The Smithsonian Institution in Washington, DC, has more than 40 million fossils—far too many to display all at once. Instead, many are stored in the museum's first floor FossiLab and others are stored in Maryland, New York City, and more sites. There are so many fossils in storage around the world that many have never been formally prepared and cataloged. Oftentimes, new species are discovered not by a fossil hunter unearthing remains in a faraway site, but by a paleontologist searching through a basement!

FOSSILS IN CRADLES

FAMOUS FOSSIL

SUE the *Tyrannosaurus rex* stands fearsomely in Chicago's Field Museum. Named after its discoverer, SUE stretches more than 40 feet (12m) long and stands 13 feet (4m) tall at the hip. It's one of the biggest *T. rex* fossils ever found! Its head is turned and its mighty jaws gape open. Scientists once thought holes in SUE's lower jaw were bite marks from a fight with another dinosaur. But now, they think the holes were likely made by a **parasite** that still infects birds today. The microscopic critters would have burrowed into the dinosaur's jaw bones, causing terrible pain and perhaps preventing SUE from eating. In fact, this infection might have been what killed mighty SUE.

SUE on display at
Chicago's Field Museum

HOLES IN LOWER JAW

DIGGING UP THE PAST
Careers in Paleontology

When you think of a paleontologist, you might picture someone digging in a hot and dusty place to unearth ancient bones. But there are many kinds of experts that study prehistoric life. Check out these lesser-known careers. Do you think you might want to become a paleontologist someday?

PALEOARTIST

Scientists can take a pile of fossilized bones and figure out how the living animal looked and behaved. But the rest of us need a little help. Enter paleoart. In this field, artists use scientific knowledge to create accurate pictures of ancient creatures. Paleoartists study the latest research on how dinosaurs looked and moved. They also have to know what the planet looked like during the Mesozoic Era, so that the plants, animals, and environment shown in their work are correct. These artists use all sorts of **media** to recreate the past: watercolors to make paintings, clay to form sculptures, and computers to build digital recreations.

CLAY SCULPTURE

PALEOBOTANIST

Animals aren't the only things that lived long ago. Scientists called paleobotanists study leaves, flowers, seeds, fruits, and other remains from ancient plants. Paleobotanists gather types of fossils called **impressions**. These are trace fossils which show a plant's shape left behind on rocks. Paleobotanists can also study bits of plants captured inside amber and other preserved remains. These fossils help paleobotanists figure out what plants grew in the world of the dinosaurs.

SLICES OF FOSSIL

2G/7RG SAMP2

2D/5PX SAMP1

THIN-SECTION SLIDES

PALEO-
PALE-ee-oh
(prefix) involving or dealing with ancient forms or conditions

PLANT IMPRESSION

PALEOECOLOGIST

It's one thing to know what forms of life inhabited Earth long ago. But how did these **flora** and **fauna** interact with one another and with their environment? That's what paleoecologists try to understand. They use fossil evidence to discover how some creatures preyed on other ones and how they competed for food and other resources. Paleoecologists also investigate how the conditions of the climate, such as temperature and rainfall, affected animals and plants of the time.

PALEOHISTOLOGIST

What do you find when you look inside a dinosaur fossil? Paleohistologists use powerful microscopes to study the patterns and arrangements of tiny structures that make up fossilized hard tissues such as teeth, eggshells, and bones. They cut a fossil into slices as thin as a human hair. Then, they look at these slices under microscopes to figure out mysteries behind the fossil, such as whether the dinosaur was a baby or an adult. Paleohistologists also investigate other types of prehistoric tissues, such as **ossified** (*AH-suh-fyde*) tendons (thin, bony rods found along the spines and tails of some dinosaurs) to explore how these animals stood and moved. All the evidence they gather helps them test **hypotheses**, or possible explanations, of how dinosaurs lived.

TAPHONOMIST

Scientists often have a lot of questions about how a dinosaur or other prehistoric animal died. But what about what happened after it died, when its bones were turning into fossils? That's where taphonomists come in. These experts study different kinds of events, including those that are **biostratinomic** (*bye-oh-strat-uh-NAH-mik*) and **diagenetic** (*dye-uh-juh-NET-ik*). Something that takes place between the animal's death and when it's buried below ground is called biostratinomic—like when scavengers tear a carcass apart and carry away some of the bones. Then, after the bones are covered by sediment, water or microbes might wear away at them. This is an example of an event that's diagenetic, which occurs after the animal has been buried by earth and rock. Taphonomists study fossils to uncover these scenarios and piece together the puzzle of exactly what happened from death to discovery.

DINOSAURS ARE STILL ALIVE!
Meet the Descendants of Dinosaurs

You won't spot a *Stegosaurus* on the way to the bus stop or have to dodge a hungry *Tyrannosaurus rex* on a camping trip. These, and almost all the rest of the dinosaurs, went extinct because of the effects of an asteroid that struck Earth 66 million years ago. But not all dinosaurs died out. In fact, it's likely that you see dinosaurs every day.

BALD EAGLE

BIRDS ARE DINOSAURS!

The avian dinosaurs, also known as birds, survived the extinction that ended the reign of the non-avian dinosaurs, or all the rest of the dinosaur species. All birds alive today are **descendants** of ancient avian dinosaurs.

WOOD STORK

SURVIVAL STRATEGIES

So, why did birds survive what 76 percent of species could not? Scientists have a lot of theories. They know that while some Cretaceous birds had teeth in their beaks, only toothless species made it through the extinction. While toothed birds were insect-eating predators, toothless birds could eat a huge variety of foods, from seeds to fruit to plants. This beak style gave them the ability to change up their diet and would have helped them make it through a time when food sources were slim. Also, the birds that survived the extinction were no bigger than ducks. Small creatures need less food, and they reproduce faster, meaning they could take over new habitats and food sources more quickly. And of course, many birds can fly. This helped them head to new locations where they could find a scrap of food or a bit of shelter.

AMERICAN WHITE PELICAN

DINOSAURS ARE ALL AROUND US

Along with snakes, lizards, frogs, mammals, and a few other creatures, birds populated the planet, adapted to new conditions, and evolved into new species. We share our home with more than 10,000 different species of these modern-day dinosaurs: from soaring eagles to flitting hummingbirds to waddling penguins. In fact, there could be a dinosaur right outside your window.

MODERN EMU

ANCESTOR
AN-sess-ter
(noun) a living thing from which another living thing is descended

DESCENDANT
dih-SEN-dunt
(noun) a living thing related to an individual or a group that lived at an earlier time

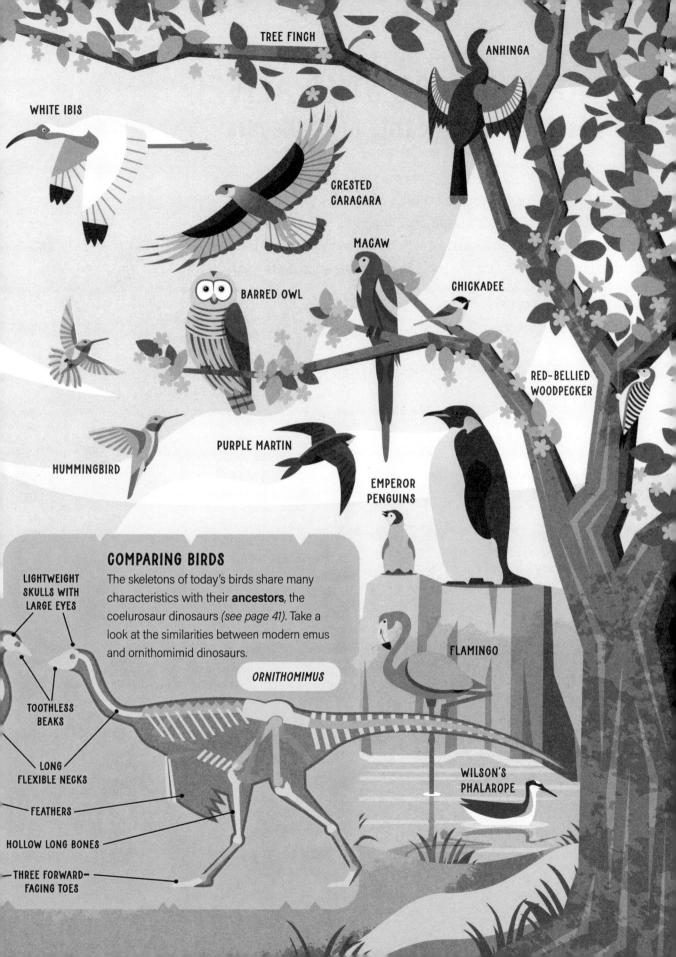

TREE FINCH

ANHINGA

WHITE IBIS

CRESTED
CARACARA

MACAW

CHICKADEE

BARRED OWL

RED-BELLIED
WOODPECKER

HUMMINGBIRD

PURPLE MARTIN

EMPEROR
PENGUINS

COMPARING BIRDS

The skeletons of today's birds share many characteristics with their **ancestors**, the coelurosaur dinosaurs *(see page 41)*. Take a look at the similarities between modern emus and ornithomimid dinosaurs.

ORNITHOMIMUS

FLAMINGO

LIGHTWEIGHT
SKULLS WITH
LARGE EYES

TOOTHLESS
BEAKS

LONG
FLEXIBLE NECKS

FEATHERS

HOLLOW LONG BONES

THREE FORWARD-
FACING TOES

WILSON'S
PHALAROPE

Paleontology Dictionary

Want to talk like a paleontologist? These **400** definitions will have you speaking the language of dinosaurs in no time.

abdomen — the part of an animal's body between the chest and the hips

absolute dating — the process of determining the real age in actual years of a rock or fossil; see also relative dating *(see page 39)*

acid — a chemical substance that when mixed with another substance (such as water) can react with other materials to promote a chemical reaction *(see page 44)*

acid rain — a type of rain that has high acidity caused by environmental factors (such as pollutants in the air) *(see page 36)*

adaptation — a modification of a body part or feature or a behavior that helps a living thing survive and function better in its environment *(see page 6)*

adhesive — a natural or artificial substance (such as glue) that can bind other substances together *(see page 44)*

age — a division of geologic time that is usually shorter than an epoch

air cell — a pocket of air inside a dinosaur egg *(see page 23)*

albumen — the white of an egg *(see page 23)*

algae — a group of plant or plantlike organisms that usually grow in water and produce chlorophyll but do not produce seeds

altricial — being hatched or born in a helpless condition or having young that are hatched or born in a helpless condition

amber — fossilized resin from long-dead trees *(see page 41)*

ammonite — any of a class of extinct cephalopods with long tentacles and a spiral shell

amnion — a thin membrane forming a closed sac around animal embryos *(see page 23)*

amoeba — a tiny water animal that is made up of a single cell

amphibian — any of a group of cold-blooded vertebrate animals (such as frogs and toads) that have gills and live in water when they are young but breathe air as adults

anatomy — the structural makeup of the body and parts of a living thing *(see page 16)*

ancestor — a living thing from which another living thing is descended *(see page 50)*

angiosperm — a flowering plant *(see page 14)*

animal kingdom — a basic group of natural objects that includes all living and extinct animals

ankylosaur — any of a group of Cretaceous plant-eating dinosaurs with bony plates covering their back

anterior — located toward the front of an animal

apex predator — an animal at the top of its food chain with few to no natural predators of its own

appendage — a part (such as a leg or branch) of an animal or plant attached to a larger or more important part *(see page 26)*

aquatic — growing, living, or done in water *(see pages 24, 34–35)*

arboreal — living in or often found in trees

archosaur — any of a class of reptiles that includes pterosaurs, crocodiles, and dinosaurs *(see page 10)*

arid — very dry and experiencing little rainfall

armature — a framework used by a museum to support a modeled figure or fossil *(see page 46)*

armor — a hard covering that protects the body *(see page 28–29)*

arthropod — any of a large group of animals (such as crabs, insects, and spiders) with jointed limbs and bodies made up of segments

asphalt pit — a naturally occurring place where asphalt seeps into Earth's surface and tends to trap animals and preserve their fossils; also known as a tar pit

asteroid — any of thousands of rocky objects in space that move in orbits and have diameters from a fraction of a mile to nearly 600 miles (1,000km) *(see pages 36–37)*

atom — the smallest particle of an element *(see page 39)*

avian dinosaur — any of a group of theropod dinosaurs that survived the Cretaceous mass extinction event and are known today as birds *(see pages 12–13, 30–31)*

bacteria — single-celled microscopic organisms *(see page 23)*

bedding — a formation of layers (strata) of sediment deposited on top of one another in sedimentary rocks

binocular — of, using, or adapted to the use of both eyes and allowing for vision in 3-D in humans and other animals

biodiversity — the existence of many different kinds of plants and animals in an environment

biogeography — a science that deals with the distribution of animals and plants around the world

biostratigraphy — the identification of fossils found within sedimentary rock layers to find out the relative age of the rock

biostratinomy — the study of events and processes that happen after an organism dies, but before it is buried *(see page 49)*

biped — an animal that walks on two legs *(see page 16)*

bivalve — an aquatic animal with a 2-valved hinged shell that is typically a marine mollusk (such as a clam, oyster, or mussel)

block — a piece of excavated rock with fossils embedded in it

body fossil — a fossil of bones or teeth that is the most commonly found kind of dinosaur remains *(see pages 40–41)*

bonebed — sediment with a lot of fossilized animal remains, including bones, teeth, and scales

brain-to-body ratio — the proportion in size of an animal's brain compared to its body *(see page 33)*

brood — to sit on or incubate eggs *(see pages 22–23)*

browse — to feed on shrubs or the leaves of trees *(see page 12)*

browser — an herbivore that feeds mostly on shrubs, shoots, leaves, and fruit

burrow — a hole in the ground made by an animal to live and shelter inside *(see page 24)*

calipers — an instrument with two adjustable arms used to measure the thickness or diameter of objects *(see page 45)*

Cambrian Explosion — the massive emergence of life forms that occurred near the beginning of the Cambrian Period during which most of the major animal groups first appeared according to the fossil record and that is one of the most important events in the history of Earth

Cambrian Period — the span of geologic time between 541 million and 485 million years ago

camouflage — to hide or disguise by covering, changing, or making harder to see

canine — a pointed tooth adapted for tearing food and usually located near the incisors, or front teeth

cannibal — an animal that eats others of its own species *(see page 27)*

carapace — a shell covering the back or part of the back of an animal (such as a turtle or crab)

carbon dating — the process of finding the age of something by measuring the amount of carbon 14 in it; also called radiocarbon dating *(see page 39)*

carnivore — an animal that feeds mostly on other animals *(see pages 20–21)*

carrion — the dead and decaying flesh of an animal *(see page 36)*

cartilage — tough flexible tissue that makes up most of the skeleton of young or developing vertebrates and, except for in a few places in the body (such as the nose or outer ear), is eventually replaced by bone

cartilaginous fish — any of a class of fishes (such as sharks, skates, and rays) that have a skeleton wholly or largely made of cartilage

cast — a reproduction of the shape of an organism's remains *(see page 46)*

catalog — to classify and document objects or specimens *(see page 47)*

caudal — directed toward or situated in or near the tail or back part of the body *(see page 16)*

cephalopod — any of a group of marine mollusks including squids, cuttlefishes, and octopuses that move by expelling water

ceratopsian — any of a group of dinosaurs of the Late Cretaceous Period having a sharp horny beak and a bony frill projecting backward from the skull *(see page 29)*

Chicxulub crater — the impact site of an asteroid that struck Earth 66 million years ago that is located off the coast of Mexico *(see page 37)*

chisel — a tool with a sharp edge at the end used to chip, carve, or cut into a solid material (such as wood, stone, or metal) *(see pages 42, 44)*

chorion — the outermost membrane around an embryo *(see page 23)*

climate — the average weather conditions of a place over a period of many years *(see page 9)*

clutch — a group of eggs laid all at once *(see pages 22–23)*

coelurosaur — any of a group of small- and medium-sized theropods whose name means "hollow-tailed reptiles" *(see page 41)*

coevolution — the process of change between two or more mutually dependent species (such as a plant and its pollinators) in which they become more and more adapted to one another as they interact

cold-blooded — see ectotherm

collagen — a protein found in the bones, muscles, skin, ligaments, and tendons of animals

cololite — the fossilized contents of the stomach *(see page 40)*

common ancestor — a species from which later species are believed to have evolved

compression fossil — a fossil that has been pressed or squeezed together and preserved in sedimentary rock

computed tomography — a process in which a three-dimensional (3-D) image of a body part or fossil is constructed by a computer *(see page 44-45)*

conifer — any of a group of mostly evergreen shrubs and trees (such as pines) *(see page 11)*

consolidant — a material that can bind and strengthen an object

continent — one of the seven sections of land on the globe: Africa, Antarctica, Asia, Australia, Europe, North America, and South America *(see pages 7, 8)*

convergent evolution — the independent development of similar looks or traits in species that are unrelated or distantly related but that live in similar environments

coprolite — fossilized dung *(see pages 20, 41)*

coracoid — a projecting part of the shoulder blade *(see pages 16-17)*

core — the hot center of Earth made up of two layers: a solid inner core and a molten (liquid) outer core

cradle — a special box with a protective lining and a foam insert with space carved out to fit a fossil specimen *(see page 47)*

crest — a showy growth (such as of flesh or feathers) on the head of an animal *(see page 19)*

Cretaceous Period — the span of geologic time between 145 million and 66 million years ago *(see pages 9, 14-15)*

crocodilian — a group of reptiles that includes living species of crocodiles, alligators, caimans, and gharials, as well as their closest extinct ancestors *(see page 35)*

crown — the top of an animal's head

crust — Earth's outermost layer, composed of separate pieces called plates

curation — the act or process of identifying and organizing artifacts and specimens

cursorial — adapted to run fast and/or for long distances *(see pages 32-33)*

cycad — any of a group of palmlike tropical plants that flourished especially during the Jurassic Period *(see page 10)*

cynodont — any of a group of mammal-like reptiles that lived from about 259 million to 100 million years ago

decay — to decrease gradually in size or quantity *(see page 39)*

deciduous tree — a tree that loses its leaves after a period of growth and use, such as in autumn

decompose — to break down or be broken down into simpler parts or substances *(see page 38)*

dental battery — rows of teeth tightly packed together to form a surface for grinding food *(see pages 32-33)*

dentary — either of a pair of bones of the lower jaw *(see page 17)*

denticle — one of the sawlike bumps on teeth that give them a serrated edge

deposition — the act or process through which sediment builds up on land by natural means (such as through wind or water)

dermal — of or relating to the skin

descendant — a living thing related to an individual or a group that lived at an earlier time *(see page 50)*

describe — to give an animal a scientific name

diagenesis — the study of processes that affect an object after burial but before fossilization *(see page 49)*

dicynodont — any of a group of plant-eating, mammal-like reptiles with beaks and tusks that lived between 270 million and 201 million years ago *(see page 10)*

digit — a finger or toe

digitigrade — walking on the toes with the back of the foot raised, as cats and dogs do

dinosaur — any of a group of mostly land-dwelling reptiles that lived millions of years ago *(see page 5)*

disarticulated — having come apart due to decay

display — a pattern of behavior (such as an animal's use of its feathers to attract a mate), especially during the breeding season

diurnal — active mostly during the day

divergent evolution — the development of different traits or features in closely related species that live in different environments

DNA — a large organic molecule that carries genetic information in the chromosomes and contains instructions about how a living thing will look and function; abbreviation of deoxyribonucleic acid *(see page 45)*

dorsal — relating to or located on the upper surface of the body of most animals (such as the dorsal fin on a *Spinosaurus*) *(see page 28)*

dromaeosaur — any of a group of fast-running, bipedal, predatory dinosaurs that lived in Asia and North America during the Cretaceous Period

duck-billed dinosaur — see hadrosaur

ecology — the study of the relationships between living things and their environment

ecosystem — the whole group of living and non-living things that make up an environment and affect each other *(see page 41)*

ectotherm — an animal (such as a fish, amphibian, or reptile) that is cold-blooded and relies on its environment to control its body temperature *(see page 7)*

edentulous — toothless

embryo — an animal in its earliest stages of growth developing inside an egg or its mother's body *(see pages 22–23)*

enamel — a hard substance that forms a thin layer capping the teeth

endemic — native to and found only in a particular place

endotherm — an animal, usually a mammal or bird, that is warm-blooded and so can control its own body temperature *(see page 7)*

eon — a very long division of geologic time, usually longer than an era

epoch — a division of geologic time that is shorter than a period and longer than an age

equator — an imaginary circle around the Earth that is everywhere equally distant from the north pole and the south pole

era — a large division of geologic time that is divided into periods

erosion — the act of wearing away (such as by water, wind, or glacial ice)

evolution — the theory that existing animals and plants have come from kinds that existed in the past

evolutionary tree — a diagram that shows the evolutionary relationships among different species from a common ancestor

excavate — to dig out and remove *(see page 42)*

exoskeleton — an external protective covering of an animal

exposure — an area of a rock formation that is visible

extant — still existing; not destroyed, lost, or extinct (such as a species)

extinction — the dying out of a species or a group of species *(see pages 8–9, 36–37)*

fauna — the animal life typical of a region, period, or special environment *(see page 49)*

fern — a class of non-flowering plants that is one of the oldest plant groups on Earth and dates back more than 350 million years *(see page 10)*

fiberglass — a lightweight material made of very thin pieces of glass that is often used to reinforce plastics and in paleontology is used as a protective covering for a fossil *(see page 46)*

fibula — the outer and smaller of the two bones between the knee and the ankle *(see page 16)*

field jacket — a protective covering made of a layer of paper towels topped with burlap bandages dipped in plaster that is placed over a specimen to keep bones and rock from falling apart *(see page 43)*

filament — a fuzzy structure that covered some dinosaurs and that eventually evolved into feathers *(see pages 18–19)*

flightless — unable to fly (like birds such as ostriches and penguins) *(see page 30)*

floodplain — low flat land along a stream that is flooded when the stream overflows

flora — the plant life typical of a region, period, or special environment *(see page 49)*

formation — a rock unit that looks different from the rock layers surrounding it and is big enough to be mapped

fossil — a trace or print or the remains of a plant or animal of a past age preserved in earth or rock *(see page 5)*

fossil record — the history of life on Earth as told through fossils and their location as preserved within layers of rock

fossiliferous — containing fossils

fossilization — the process of once-living plants and animals becoming fossils *(see pages 7, 38–39)*

frill — a growth made of bone or cartilage on the neck of an animal (such as on the backs of the skulls of ceratopsian dinosaurs) *(see page 17)*

gait — a manner or rate of movement (such as walking or running) *(see page 32)*

gastralia — an extra set of riblike bones that stretch across the abdomen of some reptiles *(see page 16)*

gastrolith — a stone eaten by an animal in order to grind up and help digest food *(see pages 20–21, 25)*

gastropod — any of a class of mollusks (such as snails and slugs) usually with a one-valved shell or no shell and a head featuring sensory organs

gene — a unit of DNA that controls the development of one or more traits in an organism and is the basic unit by which genetic information is passed from parent to offspring

genome — the genetic material of an organism

geochemistry — a science that deals with the chemical

composition of and chemical changes in Earth's crust

geologic time — the long period of time occupied by Earth's geologic history, divided into eons, eras, periods, epochs, and ages

geologist — a person specializing in the study of geology

geology — a science that deals with the history of Earth and its life, especially as recorded in rocks

ginkgo — a non-flowering tree with fan-shaped leaves that is Earth's oldest surviving tree species and that has remained largely unchanged for approximately 200 million years *(see pages 10–11)*

glacier — a large body of ice moving slowly down a slope or valley or over a wide area of land

global warming — a heating of Earth's atmosphere and oceans predicted to occur from an increase in the greenhouse effect resulting especially from air pollution *(see page 36)*

Gondwana — an ancient supercontinent that included the currently separate landmasses of South America, Africa, Arabia, Madagascar, India, Australia, and Antarctica *(see page 12)*

greenhouse effect — warming of the lower atmosphere of Earth that occurs when radiation from the Sun is absorbed by Earth and then given off again and absorbed by carbon dioxide and water vapor in the atmosphere

group — a number of living things that are considered related in some way

growth ring — markings inside an animal's bones that record growth and age *(see page 17)*

gymnosperm — a non-flowering plant that reproduces with seeds *(see page 10)*

habitatable — suitable or fit to live in

habitat — the place where a plant or animal grows or lives in nature *(see page 35)*

hadrosaur — any of a family of mainly bipedal dinosaurs of the Late Cretaceous Period that had a beaklike snout and a solid or hollow bony crest on the skull

herbivore — an animal that feeds mostly on plants *(see page 20)*

herd — a number of animals of one kind that live and/or migrate together *(see page 29)*

heterodont — an animal that has different types of teeth suited to different tasks

herpetology — a branch of zoology dealing with reptiles and amphibians

histology — the study of microscopic animal and plant tissues

holotype — a single specimen that serves as the ideal, typical, or standard model of the characteristics of that group

horn — one of the hard bony growths on the head of animals (such as ceratopsians) *(see pages 17, 19, 41)*

horsetail — a plant that produces spores and has small leaves resembling scales and whose ancestors date back 350 million years *(see page 11)*

humerus — the long bone of the upper arm or forelimb that extends from the shoulder to the elbow *(see page 17)*

hypothesis — something not proved but assumed to be true for purposes of argument or further study or investigation *(see page 49)*

ice age — a period of time during which much of Earth is covered with glaciers *(see page 35)*

ichnite — a fossil footprint *(see pages 24–25, 40)*

ichnology — the study of fossilized tracks, trails, and burrows made by animals

ichthyosaur — a prehistoric marine reptile *(see page 35)*

igneous rock — rock that is formed by the hardening of melted mineral material within the Earth

iguanodontian — any of a group of large, bipedal, herbivorous dinosaurs that lived during the Cretaceous Period

impact crater — a large depression in a planet or moon formed by a fast-traveling object from space striking the ground with great force *(see page 37)*

impression — something made by pressing or stamping against a surface *(see page 48)*

incubate — to sit on (eggs) so as to hatch by the warmth of the body

index fossil — a fossil usually with a narrow time range and wide distribution that is used in the identification of related geologic formations

insect — any of a group of small and often winged animals that are arthropods having six jointed legs and a body formed of a head, thorax, and abdomen *(see page 11)*

invertebrate — an animal without a backbone

iridescent — having the quality of shifting and constantly changing colors and producing rainbow effects *(see page 32)*

iridium — a chemical element that is common in asteroids but rare on Earth *(see page 37)*

Jacob's staff — a short square rod with a cursor used for measuring heights and distances

Jurassic Period — the span of geologic time between 201 million and 145 million years ago *(see pages 9, 12–13)*

juvenile — not fully grown or developed

keratin — a hard protein that helps form the tissues of the hair, nails, horns, scales, feathers, and outer layer of skin in animals *(see page 41)*

kingdom — one of the three basic divisions (animal kingdom, plant kingdom, mineral kingdom) into which natural objects are commonly grouped

land bridge — a strip of land connecting two landmasses

(such as two continents or a continent and an island)

latitude — the distance north or south from the equator measured in degrees

Laurasia — an ancient supercontinent that included the currently separate landmasses of North America and Eurasia except for the Indian subcontinent *(see page 12)*

law — in science, a statement (such as the law of gravity) describing something that always happens under certain conditions

Law of Superposition — a principle in geology that layers of rocks and sediment were deposited in chronological order with younger layers overlying older layers

lineage — common ancestry; the ancestors from which a species is descended

lithification — the process by which loose particles of sediment become solid rock *(see page 38)*

living fossil — an organism (such as a horseshoe crab or a ginkgo tree) that has remained essentially unchanged from earlier geologic times and whose close relatives are usually extinct

locality — a geographic area known for containing fossils

locomotion — the act or power of moving from place to place

longitude — the distance measured in degrees east or west from the prime meridian

loupe — a small magnifier

macrofossil — a fossil large enough to be observed without a microscope

mammal — a warm-blooded animal with a backbone and that feeds its young with milk produced by the mother and has skin usually more or less covered with hair *(see page 15)*

mandible — a lower jaw often with its soft parts *(see page 17)*

mantle — the layer of Earth that lies beneath the crust and above the core

marginocephalian — any of a group of dinosaurs that includes the horned-headed *Triceratops* and dome-skulled *Pachycephalosaurus*

marine — of, relating to, or living in the sea *(see pages 34-35)*

marrow cavity — the hollow inside part of the bone that contains a type of bone tissue (marrow) *(see page 17)*

mass extinction — the widespread dying out of many species in a relatively short timespan as the result of one or more triggering events

matrix — the natural material (such as rock) in which a fossil is embedded *(see page 42)*

maxilla — the upper jaw

medium — a mode of artistic expression or communication (such as painting or sculpture); plural media *(see page 48)*

melanosome — a small, pigment-filled sac inside of cells that give some body parts their color *(see pages 18-19)*

Mesozoic Era — the span of geologic time between 252 million and 66 million years ago during which dinosaurs were present and the first birds, mammals, and flowering plants appeared *(see page 9)*

metabolism — the processes by which a living organism uses food to obtain energy and build tissue and disposes of waste material

metamorphic rock — a rock formed by the action of pressure, heat, and water that results in a more compact form

meteor — an object from space that enters Earth's atmosphere and burns up before it reaches the ground

meteorite — a meteor that reaches the surface of Earth without being completely vaporized

microbe — a sometimes disease-causing organism of microscopic size *(see page 38)*

microfossil — a fossil so small it can be studied only by using special equipment (such as a microscope)

micropaleontology — the study of microscopic fossils

microscopy — the use of or investigation with a microscope

migrate — to move from one place or region to another, often on a regular basis *(see page 25)*

mineral — a naturally occurring solid substance (such as diamond, gold, or quartz) that is not of plant or animal origin *(see page 38)*

mold — the mineralized impression an organism leaves in sediment; see also cast

molecular paleontology — the extraction of organic materials from the remains of ancient plants and animals *(see page 45)*

monocular — of, involving, or affecting only one eye and providing a type of vision, especially in prey animals (such as rabbits) with eyes on opposite sides of their head, that allows animals to see potential predators approaching from both sides

morphology — the size, shape, and structure of living things *(see page 31)*

mosasaur — any of a group of large carnivorous marine lizards with limbs shaped like paddles that lived during the Cretaceous Period *(see page 34)*

natural selection — a natural process that results in the survival and reproductive success of individuals or groups best adjusted to their environment and that leads to the passing along of genetic qualities best suited to that particular environment

nature — the physical world and everything in it

nesting colony — a large group of animals of one kind living and nesting near each other at a particular location

nocturnal — active mostly at night *(see page 25)*

nodosaur — a kind of armored dinosaur that was covered in spikes but did not have a club tail *(see page 40)*

non-avian dinosaur — any dinosaur that is not a bird; see also avian dinosaur *(see page 35)*

Northern Hemisphere — the half of Earth that lies north of the equator

nothosaur — any of a group of aquatic reptiles with long limbs, necks, and tails that existed during the Triassic Period

notochord — the longitudinal flexible rod of cells that forms the supporting axis of the body in chordates

olfactory — of or relating to the sense of smell *(see page 27)*

omnivore — an animal that feeds on both animals and plants *(see pages 20–21)*

ontogeny — the development of a living thing from its beginnings (such as an egg) into an adult

organism — a living thing

ornithischian — any dinosaur whose hips were positioned like the hips of birds and that belonged to one of the two main groups of dinosaurs as distinguished by hip formation *(see page 16)*; see also *saurischian*

ornithomimosaur — any of a group of beaked dinosaurs that looked like modern-day ostriches

ornithology — the study of birds

ornithopod — any of a group of bipedal ornithischian dinosaurs (including Iguanodon and the hadrosaurs) that usually had only three functional toes

ossification — the natural process of bone formation *(see page 49)*

osteon — a cylindrical unit of bone consisting of a central canal surrounded by essential bone cells and tissues *(see page 17)*

osteoderm — a bony plate in the skin of an armored dinosaur (such as *Ankylosaurus*) *(see pages 28–29)*

overburden — the layers of rock and soil lying above a fossil *(see page 42)*

oviraptor — any of a group of bipedal theropod dinosaurs of the Late Cretaceous Period having a toothless muscular jaw, clawed finger and toes, and a crested skull and that are thought to have exhibited brooding behavior

oviparous — producing eggs (such as those of birds) that mature and hatch after they have been laid by the parent

oxygen — a chemical element found in the air as a colorless odorless tasteless gas that makes up about 21 percent of Earth's atmosphere and that is essential for life *(see page 38)*

pachycephalosaur — any of a group of herbivorous dinosaurs with thick, domed skulls

pack hunting — the behavior of predators of the same species working together to bring down prey

paedomorphosis — the retention by an adult animal of traits it had when it was very young

paleo — involving or dealing with ancient forms or conditions *(see pages 48–49)*

paleobiogeography — a science that deals with the geographical distribution of plants and animals of former geological epoch

paleobotany — the branch of paleontology that studies the fossils of prehistoric plants *(see pages 48–49)*

paleohistology — the study of ancient cells and tissue under a microscope *(see page 49)*

paleoceanography — the study of the oceans as they were in Earth's geological past

paleoclimatology — the study of the climate over periods of years of Earth's past

paleoecology — the study of the characteristics of ancient environments and their relationships to plants and animals of Earth's past *(see page 49)*

paleoenvironment — the climate, soil, and living things of a past geological age

paleogeography — the geography of ancient times or of a particular past geologic epoch

paleontologist — a person who studies life from the past using fossil remains *(see pages 5, 48–49)*

paleontology — a science dealing with the life of past geologic periods as known from fossil remains *(see page 48)*

Paleozoic Era — the span of geologic time between 541 million and 252 million years ago

palynology — a branch of science dealing with pollen and spores

Pangea — an ancient supercontinent that included almost all of Earth's land area and was formed by the collision of Gondwana and Laurasia *(see pages 8–9)*

Panthalassa — the ocean that surrounded the supercontinent Pangea; called also Panthalassic Ocean *(see page 8)*

parasite — a living thing that lives in or on another living thing and gets food and sometimes shelter from it and is usually harmful to it *(see page 47)*

pathology — the study of the essential nature of diseases and especially of the structural and functional changes produced by them

pelvis — the bowl-shaped part of the skeleton that includes the hip bones and the lower bones of the backbone

period — a division of geologic time (such as the Cretaceous Period) that is longer than an epoch and is included in an era *(see page 9)*

permafrost — a permanently frozen layer at variable depth below the surface in extremely cold regions of a planet (such as Earth)

permineralization — a process of fossilization in which mineral-rich water seeps into the pores of an organism and creates an internal cast of it

petrification — the conversion of plant or animal matter into stone or something similar to stone *(see page 38)*

petrify — to change plant or animal matter into stone or something similar to stone by replacing the matter with minerals over time *(see pages 38–39)*

phalanx — one of the digital bones of the hand or foot of a vertebrate; plural *phalanges (see page 16)*

phylogeny — the evolutionary history of a kind of living thing

physiology — the processes and activities by which a living thing or any part of it functions

photosynthesis — the process by which green plants and a few other organisms, which in the presence of light, form carbohydrates from carbon dioxide and water

phytosaur — any of a group of armored, semi-aquatic reptiles that lived during the Late Triassic Period and are distantly related to crocodiles *(see page 11)*

pigment — a coloring matter in animals and plants especially in a cell or tissue *(see page 19)*

placodont — any of a group of aquatic reptiles resembling turtles that lived during the Triassic Period

plankton — the passively floating or weakly swimming usually tiny animal and plant life of a body of water

plant kingdom — a basic group of natural objects that includes all living and extinct plants

plantigrade — walking on the sole with the heel touching the ground, as humans do

plaster — a pasty composition (usually made of lime, water, and sand) that hardens on drying and is used to make field jackets and cradles *(see page 43)*

plastron — the underside part of the shell of a tortoise or turtle

plate tectonics — a scientific theory that Earth's surface is made of very large sections that move very slowly *(see pages 8–9)*

plesiosaur — any of a group of carnivorous aquatic reptiles with long necks, small heads, short tails, wide bodies, and flippers that lived from the Late Triassic into the Late Cretaceous Periods *(see page 34)*

pliosaur — any of a group of carnivorous aquatic reptiles with short necks, large heads, and powerful jaws that lived during the Jurassic and Cretaceous Periods

pollinator — something (such as an insect) that carries small dustlike spores from a plant (pollen) from flower to flower *(see page 14)*

pore — a tiny opening, especially in an animal or plant *(see page 23)*

posterior — the area located toward the back of an animal

Precambrian Era — the span of geologic time between the formation of Earth 4.6 billion years ago and 541 million years ago

precocial — able to be independent soon after being born or hatched

predator — an animal that lives mostly by killing and eating other animals *(see page 26)*

preparator — a person who prepares scientific specimens or museum displays *(see page 44)*

preserve — to keep artifacts and fossils safe and intact for future study

prey — an animal that is hunted or killed by another animal for food *(see page 6)*

prosauropod — any of a group of plant-eating dinosaurs that lived during the Triassic Period and are probably ancestors of sauropods

prospect — to explore an area for fossils and mineral deposits *(see page 42)*

protein — a complex substance that is made up of amino acids and that is an essential part of all living cells *(see page 23)*

pterodactyl — any of various pterosaurs of the Late Jurassic and Cretaceous Periods having a primitive tail and a beak with limited teeth

pterosaur — any of a group of flying reptiles with featherless wings in the form of a thin skin that ran from the side of its body, along its arm, and ended at its long fingerlike digit *(see pages 34–35)*

pygostyle — a plate of bone found in most birds that is formed by the fused vertebrae in the tail and used to control flight *(see pages 30–31)*

quadruped — an animal that walks on four legs *(see page 16)*

quarry — an open pit usually for obtaining stone, slate, or limestone

quill knob — a bump on the surface of an animal's bone, indicating that the animal had feathers

radioactive — giving off energy in the form of rays and/or particles by the breaking apart of atoms *(see page 39)*

radiometric — of or relating to the measurement of geologic time by means of the rate of disintegration of radioactive elements

radius — the bone on the thumb side of the arm between the wrist and the elbow *(see page 17)*

raptor — a small-to-medium-sized predatory dinosaur (such as *Velociraptor*)

rauisuchian — any of a group of reptiles that were not dinosaurs and that flourished and then went extinct during the Triassic Period

relative dating — the process of determining the age of a rock or fossil compared with other materials on the geologic time scale; see also absolute age dating *(see page 39)*

reptile — a cold-blooded animal that breathes air and usually lays eggs and has skin covered with scales or bony plates *(see page 6)*

repository — a place, room, or container where something is deposited or stored

resin — a thick liquid substance that comes from trees *(see page 41)*

rodent — a usually small mammal with sharp front teeth used in gnawing

rostral — toward the mouth or nose or beak *(see page 17)*

saurischian — any dinosaur whose hips were positioned like the hips of lizards and that belonged to one of the two main groups of dinosaurs as distinguished by hip formation *(see page 16)*; see also *ornithischian*

sauropodomorph — any of a group of saurischian dinosaurs that includes sauropods and prosauropods

sauropod — any of a group of plant-eating dinosaurs that mostly walked on four legs and had long necks and tails and small heads *(see page 12)*

scale — a small, flat, and hard plate that forms part of an outer covering of an animal (such as a fish or dinosaur) *(see page 6)*

Scanning Electron Microscope (SEM) — an instrument that focuses and scans a beam of electrons over something to form an image of it

scavenge — to eat already dead or decaying material (such as other animals) *(see pages 26–27)*

scientific method — a process of questioning, investigating, and testing to gain knowledge and solve problems

sclerotic ring — a ring-shaped bone surrounding the eyeball in many fish, reptiles, and birds but not in crocodilians or mammals

scute — an external bony or horny plate or large scale; see osteoderm

sediment — material (such as stones and sand) carried onto land or into water by water, wind, or a glacier *(see page 38)*

sedimentary rock — a rock formed from sediment (such as sandstone)

serrated — notched or toothed on the edge *(see pages 20–21)*

shell — a stiff, hard covering of an animal; a firm often thin structure that contains an embryo *(see page 23)*

site — a location containing the fossilized remains of plants and/or animals *(see page 22)*

skull — the case of bone or cartilage that forms the skeleton of the head and face, encloses the brain, and supports the jaws of a vertebrate *(see page 17)*

soft tissue — the body tissue of an animal (such as muscle, fat, and blood vessels) that is not hardened and generally does not fossilize

sonic boom — a sound like a thunder made when the air-pressure waves caused by something traveling faster than the speed of sound reach the ground *(see page 18)*

species — a group of similar living things that is made up of individuals able to produce offspring with one another *(see page 6)*

specimen — a portion or quantity of material used by scientists for testing, examination, or study *(see page 44)*

spike — something shaped and pointed like a nail (such as the spikes on the tail of *Stegosaurus*)

spine — a stiff, pointed part growing from the surface of a plant or animal (such as the spines of *Spinosaurus*) *(see page 16–17)*

spinosaurid — any of a family of dinosaurs that lived during the Cretaceous Period and had sail-like structures along their back

sprawling — a posture assumed by lizards and crocodiles of holding the limbs out to the sides of the body *(see page 19)*

stegosaur — any of a group of herbivorous dinosaurs with dorsal plates and spikes that lived mostly during the Jurassic Period *(see page 13)*

stereo microscope — a tool that allows a 3-D view of a specimen *(see page 44)*

stratigraphy — geology that deals with the origin, makeup, distribution, and order of strata

stratum — a layer of rock or earth; plural strata *(see page 39)*

stromatolite — a mounded fossil that is formed from layers of cyanobacteria and that is among the planet's oldest discovered fossils

subfossil — something (such as bone) that is less than the typical fossil age but partially fossilized

supercontinent — a large landmass (such as Pangea, Gondwana, and Laurasia) from which other continents are believed to have broken off and drifted away *(see page 8)*

synapsid — any of a group of terrestrial vertebrates (such as the pelycosaurs and therapsids) that had a single pair of openings on the sides of the skull and that are considered ancestors of the mammals

talon — the claw of an animal and especially of a bird of prey *(see page 27)*

taphonomy — the study of the processes (such as burial, decay, and preservation) that affect animal and plant remains as they become fossilized *(see page 49)*

taxonomy — classification of living things (such as plants and animals) using a system that is usually based on natural relationships

tectonic plate — one of the massive slabs of rock that make up Earth's crust *(see page 8)*

terrestrial — living or growing on land

territory — an area that is occupied by or defended by an animal or a group of animals

Tethys Sea — a body of water existing from the end of the Paleozoic Era until the Cenozoic Era; called also Tethys Ocean *(see pages 8–9)*

tetrapod — a vertebrate (such as an amphibian, bird, or mammal) with two pairs of limbs

thagomizer — the cluster of spikes on the tail of a *Stegosaurus* *(see pages 28–29)*

theory — a general principle offered to explain a scientific phenomenon *(see page 8)*

therapsid — any of a group of vertebrates that flourished during the Permian and Triassic Periods and are considered ancestors of mammals

therizinosaur — any of a group of theropod dinosaurs (such as *Deinocheirus*) with long fingers and claws that lived in Asia and North America during the Late Cretaceous Period

theropod — any of a group of meat-eating dinosaurs (such as *T. rex* or *Velociraptor*) that walked on two legs, had hips positioned like those of lizards, and had hollow, long bones and usually small forelimbs *(see pages 10–11)*

thyreophoran — any of a group of armored plant-eating dinosaurs, including *Stegosaurus* and *Ankylosaurus*

tibia — the inner and larger of the two lower leg bones *(see pages 16–17)*

titanosaur — any of a group of approximately 40 species of sauropod dinosaurs, some of which were the largest animals ever known to walk the planet *(see pages 14, 32)*

topography — the natural and artificial features of a place or region

trace fossil — a fossil (such as of nests, trails, footprints, dung, or resting marks) that shows evidence of an organism's activities but is not formed from the organism itself *(see pages 40–41)*

trackway — a series of fossil footprints (such as those made by a dinosaur) *(see page 40)*

transitional fossil — a fossil that shows characteristics of its relatives of one kind that lived before and its relatives of another kind that came after *(see page 30)*

Triassic Period — the span of geologic time between 252 million and 201 million years ago *(see pages 9, 10–11)*

trilobite — any of numerous extinct marine arthropods that lived on Earth from 542 million to 251 million years ago

tsunami — a large sea wave produced especially by an earthquake or volcanic eruption under the sea; called also tidal wave *(see page 36)*

tyrannosaur — any of a group of very large meat-eating dinosaurs found in what is now North America

ulna — the bone on the little-finger side of the arm between the wrist and the elbow *(see page 17)*

ultraviolet light — a type of light invisible to human eyes *(see page 27)*

vegetation — plant life or cover (as of an area) *(see page 12)*

vertebra — one of the bony sections making up the backbone of vertebrates; plural vertebrae *(see page 16)*

vertebrate — an animal with a backbone *(see page 16)*

warm-blooded — see endotherm

weathering — the action of the weather conditions in changing the color, texture, or makeup of exposed objects

Western Interior Seaway — a large inland sea that split North America into two landmasses during the Cretaceous Period

wingspan — the distance from the tip of one wing to the tip of the other wing *(see page 13)*

yolk — the yellow inner portion of the egg of a bird or reptile that provides an embryo with nourishment *(see page 23)*

Featured Creatures

Wondering how to pronounce the dinosaurs featured in this book? Find these and the other living things that shared their world.

Dinosaurs

Alamosaurus (al-uh-moh-SOR-us) 29, 36
Allosaurus (al-uh-SOR-us) 13, 28
Anchiornis (an-kee-OR-nis) 18–19
Ankylosaurus (ang-kuh-loh-SOR-us) 29
Apatosaurus (uh-pat-uh-SOR-us) 9, 12, 18–19
Archaeopteryx (ahr-kee-AHP-tuh-riks) 13, 30–31, 41
Argentinosaurus (ahr-ghen-tee-noh-SOR-us) 7, 32–33
Avimimus (av-uh-MYE-mus) 9
Borealopelta (bor-ee-al-oh-PEL-tuh) 18, 40
Brachiosaurus (brak-ee-oh-SOR-us) 46
Camptosaurus (kamp-tuh-SOR-us) 13
Ceratosaurus (sair-uh-toh-SOR-us) 9
Citipati (sit-ee-PAT-ee) 22–23
Coelophysis (see-LOH-fuh-zis) 9, 10–11
Confuciusornis (kun-fyoo-shuh-SOR-nis) 30–31
Deinocheirus (dye-noh-KYE-rus) 21
Diplodocus (duh-PLAH-duh-kus) 12, 20–21, 46–47
Dracorex hogwartsia (DRAY-koh-reks-hahg-WAHRT-see-uh) 43
Falcatakely (fal-kah-tuh-KEL-ee) 30–31
Gargantuavis philoinos (gahr-gan-choo-AY-vis-fih-LOY-nahss) 30–31
Giganotosaurus (jye-gan-tuh-SOR-us) 20–21
Herrerasaurus (huh-rair-uh-SOR-us) 11
Ichthyornis (ik-thee-OR-nis) 14
Iguanodon (ih-GWAH-nuh-dahn) 7, 20
Kentrosaurus (ken-troh-SOR-us) 46–47
Maiasaura (mye-uh-SOR-uh) 22
Majungasaurus (muh-jung-uh-SOR-us) 27
Microraptor (MYE-kroh-rap-ter) 32
Nigersaurus (nee-jair-SOR-us) 33
Nyasasaurus (nye-ah-suh-SOR-us) 9, 10
Ornithomimus (or-nith-oh-MYE-mus) 51
Oryctodromeus (or-ik-toh-DROM-mee-us) 24
Pachycephalosaurus (pak-ih-sef-uh-loh-SOR-us) 36
Parasaurolophus (pair-uh-suh-ROH-luh-fus) 14, 19
Patagotitan (pat-uh-goh-TYE-tun) 9
Plateosaurus (plat-ee-uh-SOR-us) 9, 10
Shantungosaurus (shan-tung-oh-SOR-us) 9
Shuvuuia deserti (shuh-VOO-ee-uh-DESS-er-tye) 25
Sinosauropteryx (sye-noh-sor-AHP-tuh-riks) 7
Spinosaurus (spye-nuh-SOR-us) 7, 21, 24
Stegosaurus (steg-uh-SOR-us) 6, 12–13, 28–29
Struthiomimus (stroo-thee-oh-MYE-mus) 32–33
Triceratops (trye-SAIR-uh-tahps) 9, 14–15, 16–17, 26–27, 29
Troodon (TROH-uh-dahn) 20, 33
Tyrannosaurus rex (tuh-ran-uh-SOR-us-REKS) 6–7, 9, 15, 26–27, 29, 37, 47

Velociraptor (vuh-LAH-suh-rap-ter) 6, 27
Yutyrannus (yoo-tye-RAN-us) 18

Marine Animals

Albertonia (al-ber-TOH-nee-uh) 8
Archelon (AHR-kuh-lahn) 34
Elasmosaurus (ih-laz-muh-SOR-us) 9
Grippia (GRIP-ee-uh) 8
Ichthyosaurus (IK-thee-uh-SOR-us) 35
Plesiosaurus (PLEE-see-uh-SOR-us) 34–35
Tylosaurus (tye-loh-SOR-us) 34

Archosaurs

Batrachotomus (buh-trak-uh-TOH-mus) 8
Erythrosuchus (uh-rith-roh-SOO-kus) 8
Hesperosuchus (hess-puh-roh-SOO-kus) 11
Phytosaurus (fye-tuh-SOR-us) 11

Dicynodonts

Lystrosaurus (liss-troh-SOR-us) 8
Placerias (pluh-SEER-ee-us) 10

Pterosaurs

Pteranodon (tuh-RAN-uh-dahn) 34–35
Quetzalcoatlus (ket-sul-koh-AH-tuh-lus) 35, 37
Rhamphorhynchus (ram-fuh-RINK-us) 12

Other Reptiles

Glyptops (GLIP-tahps) 13
Coniophis (koh-nee-AH-fis) 14
Sarcosuchus imperator (sahr-koh-SOO-kus-im-PAIR-uh-tor) 35

Mammals

Alphadon (AL-fuh-dahn) 15
Castorocauda (kass-tuh-roh-KAW-duh) 35

Insects

Mormolucoides (mor-moh-loo-KOY-deez) 11

Plants

Araucarioxylon (a-raw-kair-ee-AHK-suh-lahn) 10–11
Cycad (SYE-kud) 10
Gingko (GHING-koh) 11
Magnolia (mag-NOHL-yuh) 14

APATOSAURUS

Sources

This book uses a wide range of sources to ensure that the material presented is as up to date as possible. Below is a selection of the sources used.

p. 6–7, Meet the Dinosaurs "What are Dinosaurs?" and "Dinosaurs in Argentina," www.nhm.ac.uk; "Did Dinosaurs Really Have Feathers?" www.britannica.com; "The Very First Dinosaurs," www.theguardian.com; "Dinosaurs Were Neither Cold-blooded nor Warm-Blooded, Study Finds," www.latimes.com; "Were the Dinosaurs Cold-Blooded?" www.sciencefocus.com; "Dinosaurs Started Out Hot, Then Some of Them Turned Cold," www.nytimes.com; Lambert, David, et al. *The Dinosaur Data Book* (New York: Avon Books, 1990). **p. 8–9, Earth on the Move** Brusatte, Steve. *The Rise and Fall of Dinosaurs.* (New York: Macmillan, 2018); "Mesozoic Era," kids.britannica.com; "Plate Tectonics," education.nationalgeographic.org; "Plates on the Move," www.amnh.org; "Explainer: Earth—Layer by Layer," www.snexplores.org; "Pangea," www.britannica.com. **p. 10–11, Dawn of the Dinosaurs** "Triassic Period," www.britannica.com; "The Triassic Period: The Rise of the Dinosaurs," www.nhm.ac.uk; "*Coelophysis*," www.nhm.ac.uk, www.britannica.com, www.dkfindout.com. **p. 12–13, Dinosaurs Take Over** "Jurassic Period Information and Facts," www.nationalgeographic.com; "The Jurassic Period," ucmp.berkeley.edu; "Jurassic Period," www.nps.gov; "Flowers, Pine Cones, and Dinosaurs," www.smithsonianmag.com; "Where Have the Hawk-Sized Insects Gone?" www.science.org; "How Dinosaurs Grew the World's Longest Necks," www.livescience.com. **p. 14–15, When Dinosaurs Ruled** "Did Dinosaurs Invent Flowers? (with a Big Assist from Flies and Beetles)," blog.hmns.org; "How the Earliest Mammals Thrived Alongside Dinosaurs," www.nature.com; "Cretaceous Period," www.nationalgeographic.com and natmus.humboldt.edu; "The Cretaceous Period," ucmp.berkeley.edu; "Cretaceous Period: Animals, Plants, and Extinction Event," www.livescience.com; "Flowering Plants: An Evolution Revolution," bristol.ac.uk; "Titanosaur," www.britannica.com; "A New Giant Titanosaur Sheds Light on Body Mass Evolution Among Sauropod Dinosaurs," royalsocietypublishing.org. **p. 16–17, Strong Skeletons** "So Long, SUE! Famed *T. Rex* Makes Way for Bigger Beast," www.livescience.com; "A Fresh Makeover for SUE," www.fieldmuseum.org; "Dinosaur: Classification," www.britannica.com; "Saurischia," kids.britannica.com; Sander, Martin P., et al. "Dinosaurs: Four Legs Good, Two Legs Bad," *Current Biology* 28 (2018); Cullen, Thomas M., et al. "Osteohistological Analyses Reveal Diverse Strategies of Theropod Dinosaur Body-Size Evolution," *Proceedings of the Royal Society B* 287 (2020); Horner, John R., Goodwin, Mark B., "Major Cranial Changes During Triceratops Ontogeny," *Proceedings of the Royal Society B* 273 (2005); "Dinosaur Frills Were Likely the Result of Sexual Selection," www.nhm.ac.uk; Woodward, Holly N., et al. "Growing Up *Tyrannosaurus rex*: Osteohistology Refutes the Pygmy "Nanotyrannus" and Supports Ontogenetic Niche Partitioning in Juvenile *Tyrannosaurus*," Science Advances 6 (2020). **p. 18–19, Head to Tail** "The Colors of Dinosaurs Open a New Window to Study the Past," www.smithsonianmag.com; "True-Color Dinosaur Revealed: First Full-Body Rendering," www.nationalgeographic.com; "*T. rex* Was Likely Covered in Scales, Not Feathers," www.smithsonianmag.com; "Most Dinosaurs Had Scales, Not Feathers, Fossil Analysis Concludes," www.theguardian.com; "Dinosaur's Tail Whips Could Have Cracked Sound Barrier," www.livescience.com; "Dino's Tail Might Have Whipped It Good," www.scientificamerican.com; "*Parasaurolophus*," www.dkfindout.com; "Fossilized Skull Reveals How Crested Dinosaur Got Its Fancy Headgear," www.cnn.com; Unwin, D.M., "Feathers, Filaments, and Theropod Dinosaurs," *Nature* 391 (1998); Barrett, Paul M., "Evolution of Dinosaur Epidermal Structures," *Biology Letters* 11 (2015); "What Makes a Dinosaur a Dinosaur?" www.amnh.org. **p. 20–21, On the Menu** "Herbivore Teeth and Diet," and "Carnivore Teeth and Diet," australian.museum; "Fossilized Stomach Contents Show Armored Dinosaur's Leafy Last Meal," www.reuters.com; McMillan, Dana. *History Hands On!: Dinosaur Dig* (Carthage, Illinois: Teaching & Learning Company, 2003); "Mystery Solved: Monster Dinosaur Had 8-Foot Arms, Weighed 14,000 Pounds," www.usatoday.com; Lee, Yuong-Nam, et al. "Resolving the Long-Standing Enigmas of a Giant Ornithomimosaur *Deinocheirus mirificus*," *Nature* 515 (2014); Holtz, Thomas R. Jr., "Mystery of the Horrible Hands Solved," *Nature* 515 (2014). **p. 22–23, Baby Dinosaurs** "Ancient Mongolian Nests Show that Dinosaurs Protected their Eggs," www.nature.com; "Researchers Announce World's First Dinosaur Preserved Sitting on Nest of Eggs with Fossilized Babies," carnegienmh.org; "Egg Mountain, the Two Medicine, and the Caring Mother Dinosaur," www.nps.gov; "Get to Know a Dino: *Citipati osmolskae*," and "Dinosaur Nests, Eggs, and Babies," www.amnh.org; "Dinosaur Daddies Took Care of Their Young Alone," www.nationalgeographic.com; "'Baby Dragon' Found in China Is the Newest Species of Dinosaur," www.npr.org; "Dinosaur Life Cycles: From Go to Woe," australian.museum; "Were Dinosaurs Good Parents?" www.nhm.ac.uk; "How Giant Dinosaurs Sat on Their Eggs Without Crushing Them," www.nationalgeographic.com; "Study: Dinosaurs Built Different Types of Nests for Their Eggs," www.usatoday.com; "Dinosaurs Put All Colored Birds' Eggs in One Basket, Evolutionarily Speaking," news.yale.edu; Researchers Say They've Solved the Mystery of the Missing Dinosaur Eggs," www.science.org. **p. 24–25, Dinosaur Life** "Bizarre *Spinosaurus* Makes History as First Swimming Dinosaur," www.nationalgeographic.com; "*Spinosaurus'* Dense Bones Fuel Debate Over Whether Some Dinosaurs Could Swim," www.sciencenews.org; "Tyrannosaurs May Have Hunted Together in Packs Like Wolves," www.newscientist.com; Dr. Steve Brusatte (paleontologist) in discussion with the writer, 2022; "Long-Necked Dinosaurs Migrated Hundreds of Miles, 'Stomach Stones' Reveal,'" www.livescience.com; "This Nocturnal Dinosaur Had Owl-Like Night Senses," earthsky.org; "Nocturnal Dinosaurs: Night Vision and Superb Hearing in a Small Theropod Suggest It Was a Moonlight Predator," www.discovermagazine.com; "The Dinosaurs that Dug Their Own Grave," eartharchives.org. **p. 26–27, On the Hunt** "Dinosaur Profile: *Tyrannosaurus rex* (Infographic)," www.livescience.com; Snively, Eric and Anthony P. Russell, "Craniocervical Feeding Dynamics of *Tyrannosaurus rex*," *Paleobiology* 33 (2007); "Why *Tyrannosaurus rex* Was One of the Fiercest Predators Of All Time," "Fossil Tooth Is "Smoking Gun" that *T. rex* Was a Killer," "*T. rex* Had an Amazing Sense of Smell, Gene Study Suggests," and "*T. rex*'s Tiny Arms May Have Been Used as Vicious Weapons," www.nationalgeographic.com; "*Tyrannosaurus*," www.dkfindout.com; Persons, Scott W., et al. "The Tail of *Tyrannosaurus*: Reassessing the Size and Locomotive Importance of the *M. caudofemoralis* in Non-Avian Theropods," *The Anatomical Record* 294 (2011); "Supersight for a Dino King," www.snexplores.org; "Mega-Predator *T. rex* Had Super Senses," www.amnh.org; "Obscure Dinosaur Profile #3: *Majungasaurus*," obscuredinosaurfacts.com; "The Eight Deadliest Dinosaurs," www.forbes.com; "Vicious *Velociraptor*: Tales of a Turkey-Sized Dinosaur," www.nhm.ac.uk. **p. 28–29, Powerful Protection** "Claws, Jaws and Spikes: The Science of the Dinosaur Arsenal," www.wired.com; "*Triceratops* Horns Used in Battle," "*Ankylosaurus*: Facts About the Armored Lizard," and "*Stegosaurus*: Bony Plates & Tiny Brain," www.livescience.com; "Dinosaurs: The Armoured Giants," www.theguardian.com; "Stegosaurus ungulates," www.nps.gov. **p. 30-31, Taking Flight** "Tiny Toucan-Like Bird with a Single Tooth Flew During the Dinosaur Era," www.newscientist.com; "How We Discovered a New Species of The 'Missing Link' Between Dinosaurs and Birds," theconversation.com; "O. Archaeopteryx Fossil," and "Why Are Birds the Only Surviving Dinosaurs?" www.nhm.ac.uk; "Archaeopteryx: The Transitional Fossil," and "Gigantic Birds Trod Earth During Age of Dinosaurs," www.livescience.com; "T. rex Linked to Chickens, Ostriches," www.smithsonianmag.com; "Confuciusornis," www.britannica.com; "Pygostyle," www.sciencedirect.com; "Rashid, Dana J. et al. "Avian Tail Ontogeny, Pygostyle Formation, and Interpretation of Juvenile Mesozoic Specimens," Scientific Reports 8 (2018); "The First Birds," australian.museum; "Early Bird with Tall, Sickle-Shaped Beak Reveals Hidden Diversity During the Age of Dinosaurs," www.ohio.edu. **p. 32-33, Record-Breakers** "Biggest Dinosaur Ever? Maybe. Maybe Not," and "Troodon formosus," www.nationalgeographic.com; "Argentinosuaurs," "Microraptor," and "Gallimimus," www.dkfindout.com; "Why the World's Biggest Dinosaurs Keep Getting Cut Down to Size," www.scientificamerican.com; "Microraptor," and "Troodon," kids.nationalgeographic.com; "Ornithomimidae ("Bird Mimics")," ucmp.berkeley.edu; "Ornithomimids–The Bird Mimic Dinosaurs," and "Nigersaurus," www.thoughtco.com; "Dinosaur Dads Cared For Young, Researchers Say" www.npr.org; "Nigersaurus: The 'Mesozoic Cow' with More Than 500 Teeth," animals.howstuffworks.com; "Toothy Dinosaur Mowed Earth Like Cow," www.livescience.com; "Nigersaurus," paulsereno.uchicago.edu. **p. 34-35, Dinosaur Neighbors** "What Is a Pterosaur?" www.amnh.org; "Jet-Size Pterosaurs Took Off from Prehistoric Runways," www.livescience.com; "Introduction to the Pterosauria," and "Introduction to the Ichthyosauria," ucmp.berkeley.edu; "Enormous Jurassic Sea Predator, Pliosaur, Discovered In Norway," www.sciencedaily.com; "Plesiosaur," kids.britannica.com; "Tylosaurus proriger," and "The Rise of Mammals," www.nationalgeographic.com; "How the Earliest Mammals Thrived Alongside Dinosaurs," www.nature.com; "Mosasaurs: Last of the Great Marine Reptiles," eartharchives.org; "Mosasaur: Apex Predator of the Western Interior Seaway," www.nps.gov; "SuperCroc Unleashed," australian.museum; "Prehistoric Crocodile Evolution," www.thoughtco.com; "Outlasting the Dinosaurs," www.pbs.org; "Archelon," www.britannica.com; "Ichthyosaur," www.cs.mcgill.ca. **p. 36-37, Going Extinct** Brusatte, Steve. The Rise and Fall of Dinosaurs. (New York: Macmillan, 2018); "Why Did the Dinosaurs Go Extinct?" and "Last Day of the Dinosaurs' Reign Captured in Stunning Detail," www.nationalgeographic.com; "What Killed the Dinosaurs?" www.nhm.ac.uk; "When Did Dinosaurs Become Extinct?" www.usgs.gov; "A Brief History of Dinosaurs," www.livescience.com; "Asteroid Dust Found at Chicxulub Crater Confirms Cause of Dinosaurs' Extinction," astronomy.com; "Chicxulub Crater," www.atlasobscura.com. **p. 38-39, From Bone to Stone** Bryson, Bill. A Short History of Nearly Everything. (New York: Crown, 2003); "How Do Fossils Form?" australian.museum, www.americangeosciences.org, www.livescience.com; "How Are Dinosaur Fossils Formed?" www.nhm.ac.uk; "How Do We Know How Long Ago Dinosaurs Lived?" www.amnh.org; "How Do Scientists Date Fossils?" www.smithsonianmag.org; "How SUE Became a Rock Star," www.acs.org. **p. 40-41, Amazing Evidence** "How Are Dinosaur Fossils Formed?" and "Dinosaur Footprints: How Do They Form and What Can They Tell Us?" www.nhm.ac.uk; "Incredible! Most Well-Preserved Armored Dinosaur Was a 'Spiky Tank,'" www.livescience.com; "The World's Largest Dinosaurs: Skin," www.amnh.org; "The Amazing Dinosaur Found (Accidentally) by Miners in Canada," and "First Dinosaur Tail Found Preserved in Amber," www.nationalgeographic.com; "Was the 'Sleeping Dragon' Dinosaur a Red Head?" "Tyrannosaurus Scat," and "Where Dinosaurs Walked: Eight of the Best Places to See Prehistoric Footprints," www.smithsonianmag.com; "Fossil Feathers Reveal How Dinosaurs Took Flight," www.science.org; "'Beautiful' Dinosaur Tail Found Preserved in Amber," www.bbc.com. **p. 42-43, In the Field** "How Are Dinosaur Fossils Discovered and Collected?" www.amnh.org; "How Do Paleontologists Find Fossils?" and "A Brief History of Hidden Dinosaurs," www.smithsonianmag.com; "Fossil Hunting 101," www.fieldmuseum.org; "Inside a Paleontologist's Field Kit," nhmu.utah.edu; "What Did People Think When the First Dinosaur Fossils Were Discovered?" www.scienceworld.ca; "Dragons and Dinosaurs: The Surprising Link Between Folklore and Fossils," biologos.org; "Dinosaurs and Dragons, Oh My!" shc.stanford.edu; "Meet Dracorex hogwartsia," www.childrensmuseum.org. **p. 44-45, In the Lab** "How Do Palaeontologists Remove Fossils From Rock?" www.abc.net.au; "Getting Under a Fossil's Skin: How CT Scans Have Changed Palaeontology," www.theguardian.com; "CT (Computed Tomography) Scan," my.clevelandclinic.org; Waggoner, Ben. "Molecular Palaeontology: Encyclopedia of Life Sciences," faculty.uca.edu; "Could Scientists Bring Dinosaurs Back to Life?" www.nhm.ac.uk; "Exploring the Origins of Molecular Paleontology," news.ncsu.edu. **p. 46-47, In the Museum** "The Dinosaurs on Display," www.amnh.org; "How Museums Put Dinosaurs Together," and "Bone Dry," slate.com; "Museum Fossils," www.dkfindout.com; "Which Dinosaur Bones Are "Real"?" "SUE the T. rex," and "A Fresh Science Makeover for SUE," www.fieldmuseum.org; "Which Exhibits in a Museum are Genuine?" www.theguardian.com; "Skills Lab–Fossil Restoration & Mounting," ckpreparations.com; "Fossil Lab: Curation & Preservation," www.nps.gov; "A Rare Look Inside the Smithsonian's Secret Storerooms," www.nationalgeographic.com; "FossiLab," naturalhistory.si.edu; "The Magic Behind What You'll See at the Smithsonian's New Fossil Hall," www.washingtonian.com; "The Dismantling of SUE," www.chicagotribune.com; "Sue the T. rex Is Making Big Moves With Her Big Bones," www.npr.org; "Was Mighty T. rex 'Sue' Felled By a Lowly Parasite?" news.wisc.edu; "Tallest Dinosaur Skeleton Mounted," www.guinnessworldrecords.com; "The Museum at South Kensington: Dinosaurs," and "Dippy," www.nhm.ac.uk. **p. 48-49, Digging Up the Past** "Ellen-Thérèse Lamm," museumoftherockies.org; "How Dinosaurs Are Brought Back to Life—Through Art," www.nationalgeographic.com; "Paleobotany & Paleoecology," www.cmnh.org; "Paleoecology," www.digitialatlasofancientlife.org; Organ, Chris L., "Biomechanics of Ossified Tendons in Ornithopod Dinosaurs," Paleobiology 32 (2006); " Taphonomy," www.sciencedirect.com. **p. 50-51, Dinosaurs Are Still Alive!** "These Are the Dinosaurs that Didn't Die," and "How Did Dino-Era Birds Survive the Asteroid 'Apocalypse'?" www.nationalgeographic.com; "Tiny Fossil Reveals What Happened to Birds After Dinosaurs Went Extinct," www.science.org; "A Fossil Bird in the Hand..." www.scientificamerican.com; "Why Birds Survived, and Dinosaurs Went Extinct, After an Asteroid Hit Earth," www.smithsonianmag.com.